YORK NOTE

General Editors: Professor A.N. Jeffares (University of Stirling) & Professor Suheil Bushrui (American University of Beirut)

William Shakespeare

MEASURE FOR MEASURE

Notes by John Saunders
MA (CAMBRIDGE) B PHIL (OXFORD)
*Lecturer in English Literature
University of Newcastle upon Tyne*

LONGMAN
YORK PRESS

The illustrations of the Globe Playhouse are from
The Globe Restored in Theatre: A Way of Seeing by
C. Walter Hodges, published by Oxford University Press
© Oxford University Press

YORK PRESS
Immeuble Esseily, Place Riad Solh, Beirut

ADDISON WESLEY LONGMAN LIMITED
Edinburgh Gate, Harlow,
Essex CM20 2JE, England
Associated companies, branches and representatives
throughout the world

© Librairie du Liban 1980

All rights reserved; no part of this publication may be reproduced,
stored in a retrieval system, or transmitted in any form or by any
means, electronic, mechanical, photocopying, recording, or otherwise,
without either the prior written permission of the Publishers or a
licence permitting restricted copying in the United Kingdom issued by
the Copyright Licensing Agency Ltd, 90 Tottenham Court Road, London W1P 9HE.

First published 1980
Sixteenth impression 1998

ISBN 0-582-02283-5

Printed in Singapore through Addison Wesley Longman China Limited

Contents

Part 1: Introduction	*page* 5
Shakespeare the man	5
Shakespeare and the theatre	6
Shakespeare and the age	10
A note on the text	12
Part 2: Summaries	14
A general summary	14
Detailed summaries	15
Part 3: Commentary	37
The title	37
The sources	37
Critical history	38
The characters	40
Plot and structure	48
Language	51
The play	54
Part 4: Hints for study	57
Approaching the play	57
Selecting quotations	59
Topics for study	60
Essay questions	61
Writing an essay	62
Part 5: Suggestions for further reading	65
The author of these notes	67

Part 1

Introduction

Shakespeare the man

We know almost nothing of Shakespeare's early life except that he was baptised at Holy Trinity Church, Stratford upon Avon, on 26 April 1564, and that he married Ann Hathaway at the end of 1582. Since his father, a glove-maker and business man of some standing in the town, had connections with the local grammar school, it is reasonable to assume that Shakespeare attended there and received the Latin-based education of the day. Records show that his father's fortunes declined after about 1577, and Shakespeare may have had to leave school early. Apart from his marriage to Ann, the birth of a daughter in May 1583 and of twins the following year, we know nothing of him until 1592, when it seems he was already established in London as an actor and playwright. In the intervening years we may, if we wish, imagine him poaching deer on the estate of Sir Thomas Lucy, as legend has it, or teaching as a country school-master, or more probably joining a provincial theatrical company and so finding his way to the capital in the late 1580s.

Since the first biography of Shakespeare, by Nicholas Rowe, did not appear until 1709, long after the death of anyone who could have known the poet personally, for his life outside the theatre we have to rely on town records, legal documents and the like. From these we know that by the late 1590s he was wealthy enough to buy property including New Place, a large house in Stratford. His family probably remained in the town, and Hamnet, his only son, died there in 1596. Shakespeare retired to spend his last years in Stratford and on 25 April 1616 he was buried in the church where he had been baptised fifty-two years before.

To add some colour to the factual record, Shakespeare's works are often pressed for biographical information. In 1593 he published a long poem, *Venus and Adonis*, and dedicated it to the Earl of Southampton. The following year another poem, *The Rape of Lucrece*, probably written while the theatres were closed because of the plague, was also dedicated to Southampton. We know a good deal about the Earl, who was ten years younger than the poet, but nothing of any connection between them beyond these dedications. Shakespeare's sonnets were not printed until 1609, though most of them appear to date from the 1590s, and attempts to see the dedicatee, 'Mr W. H.', as Southampton are unconvincing. Indeed the dedication may be the publisher's rather than the author's, and centuries of scholarship have been unable to identify either Mr W. H., or the noble youth to whom the bulk of the sonnets are addressed, or the 'Dark Lady' who appears in some of the later ones. Some of them have been associated with the troubled mood supposedly behind the plays written round the turn of the century, and sonnets like number 94 with its famous last line may make us think of *Measure for Measure*: 'Lilies that fester smell far worse than weeds.' Yet the sonnet and the sonnet sequence were highly artificial forms and Shakespeare the private individual is no more visible here than in the plays. It is because he wrote the plays that Shakespeare the man continues to fascinate us.

Shakespeare and the theatre

The company with which Shakespeare is particularly associated was known as the Lord Chamberlain's Men until 1603 when James I, the new king, became their patron, and, as the recognised leaders in their profession, they became known as the King's Men. All Shakespeare's plays were written with these actors in mind and to demonstrate their skills. To take an example, the change in the nature of the clowns' roles before and after 1599 is generally explained by the fact that Will Kempe, who specialised in acrobatic comedy, was succeeded in that year by Robert Armin, a 'wise fool' noted for his singing. Shakespeare himself was both writer and actor, and as late as 1603 he is listed as one of the company acting in Ben Jonson's *Sejanus his Fall*. He was also a ten per cent shareholder when the Globe Theatre was erected in 1599.

Although Shakespeare's plays were performed in a number of London theatres he is associated above all with the Globe, until one of his plays literally brought the house down. In 1613 cannon used in a performance of *Henry VIII* set fire to the thatched roof and the building was destroyed. We have no details of the dimensions of the theatre but surviving records for other houses give us the main features. Three galleries ran round an open courtyard into which the stage projected more than twenty feet, so that the 'groundlings', those members of the audience who paid for standing room only, surrounded it on three sides. Wealthier patrons occupied the galleries and the total audience may have been as many as three thousand. The stage itself was head-high, to allow for trap-doors, and covered by a canopy. At the back was the 'tiring house' where the actors changed and from which they made their entrances. Another gallery along the front of the tiring house provided a raised area when needed, as for the balcony scene in *Romeo and Juliet*. Curtains underneath offered concealment; no doubt the Duke stood there to overhear Claudio and Isabella in Act III Scene 1 of our play.

The open stage demanded the kind of 'theatre-in-the-round' which has re-emerged only in the last few decades. An actor might be closer to the audience than to his fellow actors upstage (at the back of the stage; the part nearest the audience is 'downstage'), so that the many soliloquies and asides found in Shakespeare's plays were a natural consequence of the physical situation. The absence of a front curtain meant that the action probably flowed without interruption and elaborate fixed scenery was not possible, though there were more 'props' (the movable 'properties' such as chairs and tables, needed in the course of the play's action) and special effects than was once believed. Surviving inventories

THE GLOBE PLAYHOUSE

The theatre, originally built by James Burbage in 1576, was made of wood (Burbage had been trained as a carpenter). It was situated to the north of the River Thames on Shoreditch in Finsbury Fields. There was trouble with the lease of the land, and so the theatre was dismantled in 1598, and reconstructed 'in an other forme' on the south side of the Thames as the Globe. Its sign is thought to have been a figure of the Greek hero Hercules carrying the globe. It was built in six months, its galleries being roofed with thatch. This caught fire in 1613 when some smouldering wadding, from a cannon used in a performance of Shakespeare's *Henry VIII*, lodged in it. The theatre was burnt down, and when it was rebuilt again on the old foundations, the galleries were roofed with tiles.

8 · Introduction

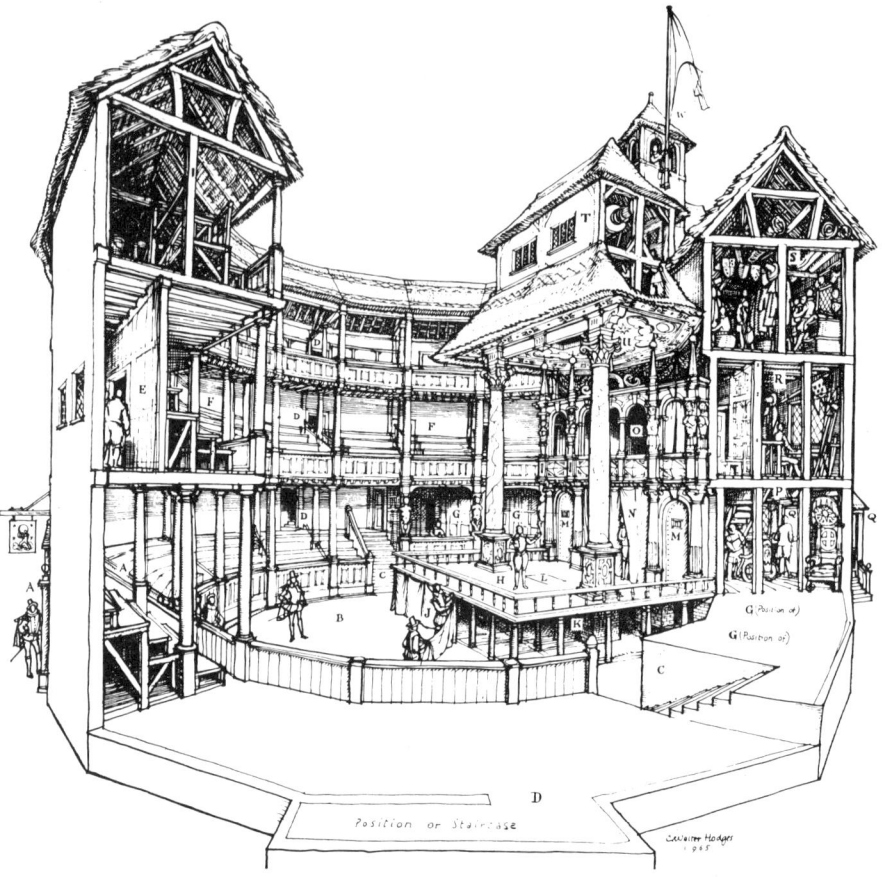

A CONJECTURAL RECONSTRUCTION OF THE INTERIOR OF
THE GLOBE PLAYHOUSE

- AA Main entrance
- B The Yard
- CC Entrances to lowest gallery
- D Entrance to staircase and upper galleries
- E Corridor serving the different sections of the middle gallery
- F Middle gallery ('Twopenny Rooms')
- G 'Gentlemen's Rooms or Lords Rooms'
- H The stage
- J The hanging being put up round the stage
- K The 'Hell' under the stage
- L The stage trap, leading down to the Hell
- MM Stage doors
- N Curtained 'place behind the stage'
- O Gallery above the stage, used as required sometimes by musicians, sometimes by spectators, and often as part of the play
- P Back-stage area (the tiring-house)
- Q Tiring-house door
- R Dressing-rooms
- S Wardrobe and storage
- T The hut housing the machine for lowering enthroned gods, etc., to the stage
- U The 'Heavens'
- W Hoisting the playhouse flag

show that in 1598 one of the rival companies possessed a 'tree of golden apples', two 'moss banks', and a 'chain of dragons', and presumably the Lord Chamberlain's Men were not to be outdone in this department.

Since women were not allowed on the public stage, all female roles were played by boys. No doubt this was a limitation, but Shakespeare's plays still give us some of the world's most famous love stories. Suggestions that a highly stylised kind of acting must have been used by men and boys alike probably underestimate the ability of the specially trained boy actors. The acting may have differed from what we know today, but the relatively intimate nature of the theatre and the range of Shakespeare's verse point to something no less powerful. In Richard Burbage the company possessed the leading actor of his day and the creator of most of Shakespeare's tragic heroes. Hamlet's advice to the players shows that by 1601 Burbage and his fellows were not content to bawl the lines:

> Nor do not saw the air too much with your hand, thus; but use all gently: for in the very torrent, tempest, and – as I may say – whirlwind of passion, you must acquire and beget a temperance, that may give it smoothness. (*Hamlet*, III.2.4–9)

In 1608 the King's Men took a second theatre at Blackfriars and played the winter season there; again Shakespeare was one of the seven shareholders. The building was much smaller than the Globe, the audience more select, and indoor lighting was required. Some of the changes in Shakespeare's late romances such as *The Tempest* and *The Winter's Tale* may be explained by the move, although the company continued to use the Globe as well. The new fashion for the Court Masque with elaborate machinery and effects, developed by the architect Inigo Jones, must have counted for something too.

The theatre had come a long way from the comedies, moralities and chronicle plays which held the stage when Shakespeare arrived in London and Christopher Marlowe (1564–93) was the leading dramatist of the time. Yet the conventions established in those early years lie behind all Shakespeare's work. In 1578, two years after the opening of the first London theatre, in the preface to *Promos and Cassandra*, the primary source for *Measure for Measure*, George Whetstone listed them as follows:

> For to work a comedy kindly, grave old men should instruct: young men should show the imperfections of youth: Strumpets should be lascivious: Boys unhappy: and Clowns should speak disorderly: intermingling all these actions, in such sort, as the grave matter, may instruct: and the pleasant, delight: for without this change, the attention would be small: and the liking, less.

Shakespeare and the age

Though the plays may not give us Shakespeare the man, they do give us the times in which he lived. He was the most successful of dramatists because his plays held the mirror up to a nature which his contemporaries recognised and shared. The audience at the Globe may have included the men and women who went to a bear-baiting the day before, but they came to the theatre with different expectations. The theatrical profession was scarcely respectable, and Shakespeare's company was often persecuted by the puritan Lord Mayor of London, but the drama had its defenders who could argue their case by referring to Greek and Latin authorities and to the parables of Christ. In 1595 Sir Philip Sidney (1554–86)'s *An Apologie for Poetrie* defined the dramatic poet as 'indeed the right Popular Philosopher'.

Popular philosophy mingled with entertainment in the collection of tragedies reprinted from the 1550s onwards as *A Mirror for Magistrates* to which *Measure for Measure* might almost be an appendix and Angelo an example of the need for temperance described by one of the authors there: 'For to covet without consideration: to pass the measure of his degree: and to let will run at random, is the only destruction of all estates.' The debate over justice and mercy which we read in Shakespeare's play is not an invention of later critics, but intrinsic to his whole conception and would have been recognised as such by the first audiences.

When Berthold Brecht (1898–1956) produced his version of *Measure for Measure* he turned it into a radical critique of a society where justice gave way to wealth and class. Although Shakespeare was no mere apologist for the status quo, what he gives us is quite unlike Brecht and much closer to the view of the French philosopher Montaigne (1533–92), whose essays were translated into English in 1603: 'There is, in public affairs, no state so bad, provided it has age and stability on its side, that is not preferable to change and disturbance.' *(Essays,* II.xvii)

Medieval certainties still underpinned Elizabethan society, although changes there inevitably were, in politics, in religion, and in the sciences. The deeper notes sounded in the plays of Shakespeare's maturity no doubt reflect these changes, but a picture of Elizabethan optimism and exuberance giving way to Jacobean despair is too simple. In 1600 the Earl of Essex's rebellion was easily defeated, and when James I came to the throne the problem of the succession at last seemed solved. It can hardly be claimed that when Elizabeth I died 'a whole civilisation lay in ruins', though tensions within that civilisation were to come to a head not long after Shakespeare's death. The ruler was still regarded as the apex of a structure which reflected the divine order underlying the universe, and James I was very conscious of his position. In 1603 his book *Basilikon Doron*, ('The King's Gift') was published in London, setting out the qualities required of the ideal ruler, and it has been suggested that *Measure for Measure,* presented at court on 26 December 1604, was written with the King in mind. In fact James was restating traditional commonplaces, though they did not always accord with the reality of the relationship between the Stuart monarchy and an evolving parliament. In Shakespeare's play the Duke's departure leads to disorder which is only resolved when he resumes his rightful place as head of state.

The Bible can be claimed as one of the sources for *Measure for Measure* with more plausibility than the *Basilikon Doron,* though it is unlikely that Shakespeare wrote with either book in front of him. We know nothing of the strength or colour of his religious beliefs, but he lived at a time when religion provided the moral language with which men defined their place in the world. The drama echoes St Matthew not because Shakespeare set out to turn the Sermon on the Mount into a play, but because the play raises questions to which the Christian religion had memorably addressed itself, in terms that had become part of the common heritage. It is true that the censorship of the period would have prevented more explicit treatment of religious themes, but there is no sign that Shakespeare felt this as a restriction. Although Angelo finds the Duke's knowledge of his sins 'like power divine', it is based on human powers of observation and results in a tolerance compounded of Christian and classical influences.

Christianity taught the importance of man's soul, but the men of Shakespeare's day drew on the Greek and Latin philosophers in their attempts to understand its connection with the body. Physiology and psychology were linked; the body, composed of the four elements, related in turn to the four humours of the blood, was animated by the natural, vital, and animal spirits. The soul itself had three powers, the vegetable, sensible, and reasonable, ideally working in harmony but potentially in conflict. Our century has given us new concepts for describing these conflicts, though vestiges of the earlier system remain in our language when we use words like 'sanguine' or 'phlegmatic'. Such a system explained the violent changes of personality so convenient for the dramatist, and gave the opposition of passion and reason a more than metaphorical force. Angelo could complain with Shakespeare's Othello:

    Now, by heaven,
My blood begins my safer guides to rule;
And passion, having my best judgement collied,
Assays to lead the way. (*Othello* II.3.204–7)

Many of the ideas of his time Shakespeare must have held quite unconsciously, but he also had a dramatist's instinct for live issues. We can trace the conventions out of which the plays are constructed – disguised dukes, for example, figure in the work of several of his contemporaries – but these are only the bare bones of the living whole. The Duke in *Measure for Measure* who 'contended especially to know himself' has something of Shakespeare's own interest in the difference between what people appear to be and the secret self which becomes clear only in the course of their actions. This underlying reality is always problematic, demanding sympathy rather than satire. Shakespeare does not move, like Bacon's philosopher,* from doubts to certainties, but only to the kind of resolution that a play can offer.

A note on the text

Elizabethan playwrights wrote for the stage rather than the page, and publication was by no means the rule. Only sixteen of Shakespeare's plays were printed during his lifetime, and *Measure for Measure* was not among them. Although it was first acted in 1604, it was not until his fellow actors, John Heminges and Henry Condell, collected the plays in 1623 that a text was available to the reader. By then Shakespeare had been dead seven years, and for their edition, the First Folio, Heminges and Condell drew on those plays already published in the Quartos (the size of paper supplies the names by which the editions are known) and on promptbooks and manuscripts probably left with the theatre company to which they and Shakespeare belonged.

In the case of *Measure for Measure* it has been suggested that a scribe copied Shakespeare's rough draft or 'foul papers', and that this copy then went to the printers, where four compositors set it up in type. Such a process would almost inevitably result in mistakes and inconsistencies, even if the original manuscript were faultless, and indeed there are mistakes in *Measure for Measure,* particularly in Act II Scene 2. Luckily most of them are not noticeable in the theatre, but even so they have led some editors to argue that the play must have been substantially revised during the nineteen years before 1623. Shakespeare may well have revised his plays, but there is no evidence that *Measure for Measure* was ever very different from the text we read.

Since there is no earlier printing, all modern editions derive ultimately from the First Folio of 1623. Later editions have supplied additional

---

*Sir Francis Bacon (1561–1626) became Lord Chancellor under King James; he is best remembered for his *Essays* in which he pioneered the inductive method of reasoning. He saw philosophy as the open-minded approach to particular problems, general conclusions only following when the evidence had been weighed. The phrase used here is based upon a quotation from Bacon's *The Advancement of Learning*: 'If a man will begin with certainties, he shall end in doubts; but if he will be content to begin with doubts, he shall end in certainties' stage directions and scene headings. The Folio Dramatis Personae gives the scene as 'Vienna' but there are no other indications of place. Punctuation and even the words have been altered, not always with happy results. One example from *Measure for Measure* will illustrate the problems involved. In Act III Scene 1 at line 93, when Claudio hears of Angelo's demand that Isabella give up her virginity to save his life, he exclaims 'The prenzie Angelo!' Since 'prenzie', the word in the First Folio, is unknown in modern English, editors either let it stand with some kind of explanation – it derives from the Italian for 'prince', or is a colloquial term meaning 'prissy' or 'prudish' – or substitute another word. The Second Folio of 1632 printed 'princely'; and 'priestly' and 'phrenzied' are other possibilities, as is 'precise', a word used by the Duke to describe Angelo in the previous act. Good modern editions usually note the creative suggestions of earlier editors, so that the reader can choose for himself.

In these notes, the edition followed throughout is the New Arden, edited by J. W. Lever, Methuen, London, 1965.

Part 2

Summaries
of MEASURE FOR MEASURE

A general summary

Vincentio, Duke of Vienna, announces his intention to leave the city for a time and travel to Poland. During his reign the law has fallen into neglect, and vice is widespread. Rather than carry out the necessary reforms himself he appoints a deputy, Angelo, to administer the city in his absence.

The first victim of the new regime is Claudio, a young nobleman who has made Juliet, the girl he is to marry, pregnant. On his way to prison he meets a dissolute friend, Lucio, and explains that his offence is punishable by death. His only hope is that his sister Isabella may persuade the deputy to mercy, and he asks Lucio to take a message to her.

We now learn that the Duke has not left Vienna but is to remain, disguised as a friar, so that he can observe the effects of his plan and in particular the behaviour of Angelo. Lucio finds Isabella, who is about to enter the religious order of St Clare, and tells her of her brother's danger.

Meanwhile Escalus, Angelo's fellow deputy, also pleads for Claudio, but without success. When he himself has to administer the new laws he gives the offenders a second chance. Angelo declares that he is ready to be judged by the same high standards he expects from others, and this is the line he takes when Isabella comes to see him. Without wishing to excuse her brother's fault she argues for mercy, while Angelo insists that justice can allow no exceptions. The only result of her efforts is that Angelo is sexually aroused by her purity.

The Duke goes to the prison where he talks to Juliet and learns of her love for Claudio, who is to be executed next morning. Isabella returns for a second interview with Angelo, who offers her her brother's life in return for her virginity. Horrified, she threatens to expose him, but he warns her that no one will believe her accusations.

At the prison the Duke in his disguise as friar offers Claudio the consolations of philosophy and leaves him ready to die bravely. Isabella arrives and is dismayed when her brother clutches at the chance to live, even at the price of her honour. She turns angrily on him for his cowardice. The Duke, who has overheard the conversation, stops her as she leaves, and reveals a plan to save Claudio's life and unmask Angelo. It will also help Mariana, a young woman contracted to marry Angelo until the partial loss of her dowry led him to break the engagement. The plan is that Isabella should accept Angelo's offer, but that Mariana should go to his bed in her place under cover of darkness. Once the marriage is consummated, Angelo will be unable to deny it.

Isabella and the Duke get Mariana's consent to their scheme and all goes as planned except that Angelo breaks his promise to free Claudio. The Duke is at the prison expecting the pardon when an order for execution comes instead, but he gets the Provost to substitute for Claudio's head that of another prisoner who has recently died. However, he tells Isabella her brother is dead, and advises her to appeal for justice to the Duke who is to return the following day.

She does so, but the Duke appears to believe Angelo's denials, even when Mariana adds her story to Isabella's. He gives Angelo permission to investigate the matter, while he leaves them. 'Friar Lodowick', the role the Duke has adopted and which he now resumes, is summoned to explain his part in the business.

The supposed friar speaks out against the corruption of the city, criticising even the Duke. Angered for their different reasons, Escalus, Angelo and Lucio turn on him, and his disguise is pulled aside. Seeing that he can no longer conceal his crimes, Angelo confesses, and asks to be executed. First, the Duke says, he must marry Mariana, and then, in spite of her protests, he must die. At this point Isabella intervenes to beg mercy for the man she thinks has caused her brother's death. The Duke can now let it be known that Claudio is still alive; he is duly pardoned, and Angelo too. It seems the Duke's mercy will not extend to Lucio, who has slandered him throughout the play, but he is condemned only to marry the girl who has borne his child. The pattern of marriages is completed when the Duke turns to Isabella and asks for her hand.

Detailed summaries

Act I Scene 1

The Duke has announced his intention to leave Vienna, placing the government of the city in the hands of two deputies. One of these, Escalus, has long experience of the necessary skills, but the main responsibility is to go to Angelo, a younger man with an outstanding reputation for virtue. This virtue, the Duke tells Angelo, is now to be seen in action. Angelo is reluctant, but the Duke has made up his mind; Angelo is to have absolute power. The Duke hurries out, leaving the deputies to discuss their new duties.

NOTES AND GLOSSARY:
Like Escalus, the Duke seems sure of Angelo's ability and his appointment is the result of considerable reflection: 'we have with

16 · Summaries

special soul/Elected him, (line 17). Yet his characterisation of Angelo warns us that there may be something self-regarding and suspect in his virtue:

> Heaven doth with us as we with torches do,
> Not light them for themselves; for if our virtues
> Did not go forth of us, 'twere all alike
> As if we had them not. (lines 32-5)

We see that Angelo is instructed 'so to enforce *or qualify* the laws/ As to your soul seems good' (lines 65-6). Mercy is to temper justice.

Critics have connected the Duke's distaste for the 'loud applause' (line 70) of the common people with similar sentiments expressed by James I as evidence that Shakespeare had the King in mind when creating his Duke. But in any case, since, as we learn in Act I Scene 3, the Duke is not in fact leaving the city, an unobtrusive departure best suits his plans.

properties: qualities
science: knowledge
lists: limits
pregnant: well informed
belongings: attributes
use: return for investment
bend: direct
Mortality: death
Aves: acclamations

Act I Scene 2

Lucio is in conversation with two gentlemen when Mistress Overdone comes in with news of Claudio's arrest. Her servant Pompey follows with details of the proclamation which has led to the arrest and will close the brothels on which their living depends. Claudio himself enters on his way to prison, led by the Provost and accompanied by Juliet. Lucio learns that Claudio's crime is getting Juliet with child, an offence punishable by death, though their marriage lacks only the formality of a religious ceremony. Angelo has revived a forgotten law, perhaps to make his presence felt in his new office, so Claudio suggests. He asks Lucio to take the news to his sister Isabella and to get her to intercede with Angelo.

NOTES AND GLOSSARY:
The conversation with which the scene opens exists mainly for its bawdy humour, but in illustrating the gap between public morality and private behaviour it is relevant to the theme of the play. Many of the jokes

concern venereal disease, a reminder that the proclamation may have something to be said for it. Claudio is not promiscuous, but, as Mistress Overdone tells the others, 'worth five thousand of you all' (line 57).

In Elizabethan law a promise of marriage made before witnesses had legal force, although the church required an additional ceremony.

Claudio's hopes of his sister's success with Angelo depend on her verbal skill, 'reason and discourse' (line 175), and the more general persuasive powers of her youth and beauty.

composition:	agreement
table:	list
raz'd:	erased
grace:	prayer before meals, also divine mercy
list:	border of a piece of cloth
kersey:	coarse woollen cloth
piled:	(cloth) with a nap
pilled:	stripped (of hair)
Madam Mitigation:	as the keeper of a brothel Mistress Overdone alleviates, or mitigates, sexual appetite
dolours:	coins, also sorrows
crown:	coin, also top of the head (made bald by syphilis)
sweat:	bubonic plague
custom-shrunk:	short of customers
maid:	virgin, also young fish
The words of heaven:	the Bible (possibly referring to Romans 9:15–18 which seems to be paraphrased here)
fast:	abstinence
ravin:	eat ravenously
bane:	poison
as lief:	rather
denunciation:	public announcement
meet:	right
glimpse:	gloss
stagger:	be uncertain
nineteen zodiacs:	nineteen years
tickle:	insecurely
tick-tack:	game in which pegs were put into holes, and so an allusion to sexual intercourse

Act I Scene 3

The Duke tells Friar Thomas his reasons for staying in Vienna, disguised as a friar. He wishes to tighten up the laws, but a sudden change of policy might seem arbitrary and unjust. Angelo will be able to

18 · Summaries

make a new start. It will also give the Duke a chance to see if his deputy is really the incorruptible figure he seems.

NOTES AND GLOSSARY:

The Duke's decision may seem questionable, as though he were evading the consequences of his own negligence in asking Angelo to take over. The text at this point (lines 41–3) is rather obscure, but probably the Duke is less concerned for his own reputation than for the dignity of his office, on which the good order of the city depends, and which may be open to slander if he is personally involved. As the new broom, Angelo will be able to sweep clean.

His other reason for stepping down, to test Angelo, although given as secondary, is the one that will occupy him for the rest of the play. Whatever the Duke's reasons for his actions, Shakespeare shows no inclination to criticise them. He is more interested in getting on with the story of Angelo and Isabella.

dribbling: feeble
complete: invulnerable
bravery: ostentation
stricture: strictness
athwart: awry
in th'ambush: under cover
sway: rule

Act I Scene 4

Isabella, who is about to enter a convent, hears from Lucio of her brother's arrest, and also something of Angelo whom she must move to pity. She agrees to try.

NOTES AND GLOSSARY:

Just as the Duke calls Angelo from the private cultivation of his virtue to direct contact with humanity, so Lucio summons Isabella from the very door of the convent. Her wish for the 'more strict restraint' (line 4) of the religious order matches Angelo's opposition of 'study and fast' (line 61) to the 'motions of the sense' (line 59) and his appetite for 'the rigour of the statute' (line 67). They are two puritans who know little of the world or themselves, although quick to condemn the weaknesses of others.

votarists of Saint Clare: an order of nuns dedicated to St Clare, founded at Assisi in Italy in 1212
stead: help
to seem the lapwing: to act deceitfully
enskied: heavenly
Fewness: to be brief

seedness:	state of being sown
teeming foison:	abundant harvest
tilth and husbandry:	cultivation
Bore . . . in hand:	deceived
giving out:	stated intentions
snow-broth:	melted snow
rebate:	dull
heavy sense:	severe application
my pith of business:	the essence of my business
owe:	own
the Mother:	the head of the convent

Act II Scene 1

Escalus defends Claudio as a young man of good family and asks if Angelo himself might not have offended in the same way in Claudio's circumstances: "'Tis one thing to be tempted, Escalus,/Another thing to fall'/, (lines 17–18). Angelo answers. The law judges men's deeds and not their thoughts. Escalus gives way and orders are given for Claudio's execution 'by nine tomorrow morning' (line 34).

They turn their attention to another case brought by Elbow, a constable, involving his wife, whom it seems Pompey has attempted to procure for Master Froth, 'a foolish gentleman'. Angelo leaves the matter to his fellow deputy who, unable to untangle Elbow's confused story, lets them all off with a caution. Escalus then goes to his dinner, his thoughts once more with Claudio.

NOTES AND GLOSSARY:

Escalus's efforts to persuade Angelo foreshadow Isabella's in the next scene, and later events will bring out the irony in Angelo's answers. Shakespeare is fascinated by the fact that society must have laws, but that the laws can only be administered by fallible men.

Angelo has condemned Claudio, and we now have a chance to see Escalus dealing with a case of sexual misdemeanour. If Angelo is too severe it is tempting to see Escalus as too lax, but in asking Elbow to bring him the names of some six or seven men to serve as constables he is at least taking steps to see that the law is more effectively maintained in the future.

Elbow with his malapropisms recalls a more famous constable, Dogberry in Shakespeare's *Much Ado about Nothing,* who has the same difficulty with words.

Pompey's part in the scene is more significant. Whereas for Angelo the law is an impersonal absolute, for Pompey it is an arbitrary human invention. Even the trade of bawd would be lawful 'if the law would allow it' (line 224). The law must take account of human nature as it is, and not as it might be in a better world. The new proclamation will surely fail unless the authorities 'geld and splay all the youth of the city' (lines 227-8). Although he cannot admit it, Escalus no doubt agrees.

fear:	frighten
strait:	strict
blood:	sexual desire
pregnant:	clear
For:	because
come in partial:	be allowed in my favour
pilgrimage	life
Some run from brakes of ice and answer none:	an obscure line. If this reading is correct it may mean 'some escape the icy torments reserved in hell for those guilty of sexual offences'
common houses:	brothels
lean upon:	rely upon, with a pun on the constable's name, Elbow
profanation:	contemptuousness (throughout this interview Elbow says the opposite of what he means)
out at elbow:	at a loss
parcel:	part-time
hot-house:	bath-house, but often the cover for a brothel
detest:	protest, Elbow means to say
Marry:	indeed
cardinally:	carnally, he means
misplaces:	mixes up his words
stewed prunes:	a dish associated with prostitutes
Go to:	get on with it
wot:	know
All-hallond Eve:	Hallowe'en, 31 October
Bunch of Grapes:	name of a room in the inn
respected:	suspected, he means
caitiff:	coward
varlet:	rascal
Hannibal:	cannibal, he means
took you a box o' th' ear:	slapped your ears
draw:	tapsters drew drink from the cask, but execution by hanging was sometimes accompanied by 'drawing' (disembowelling). Escalus is warning Froth to change the company he keeps
geld and splay:	castrate and sterilise
drab:	cheap prostitute

Summaries · 21

Pompey the Great: Roman general (106–48BC) defeated by Julius Caesar (c. 102–44BC) at the Battle of Pharsalus in Greece. The size of Pompey's buttocks or 'bum' prompts the joke
head: behead
bay: part of a house under one gable
Mercy is not itself that oft looks so: mercy too often exercised becomes mere licence

Act II Scene 2

The Provost asks if Claudio must really die tomorrow, and if so what is to be done with Juliet who is soon to give birth. Typically, Angelo answers that she must be looked after, but not made too comfortable. Isabella enters and urged on by Lucio begins to plead for her brother. Rulers should show mercy, she argues. Christianity teaches that all men are sinners, yet God is merciful. Is Angelo himself so much better than Claudio?

> Go to your bosom,
> Knock there, and ask your heart what it doth know
> That's like my brother's fault. (lines 137–9)

Angelo appears to feel the force of this and asks her to come back next morning. Left alone he examines his motives. Isabella's virtue arouses sexual feelings where a more obviously seductive woman would leave him unmoved. For the first time he recognises the disturbing power of passion.

NOTES AND GLOSSARY:
Since Isabella shares Angelo's view of sexual licence she finds it difficult to begin: 'I am/At war 'twixt will and will not' (lines 32–3). Underlying her argument is the familiar biblical text 'Judge not, that ye be not judged' (Matthew 7.1), but as she goes on she becomes more personal, moving from justice in general to Angelo in particular. Angelo resists this: 'It is the law, not I, condemn your brother' (line 80), but eventually gives way. The irony of the situation is that in appealing to the man beneath the judge's robes she has released those sexual impulses she is unable to control. Angelo is moved, but not to love. He sees Isabella's virtue as a means to trap him, the most effective means, though she could not have known it:

> O cunning enemy, that, to catch a saint,
> With saints dost bait thy hook! (lines 180–1)

He recognises the perversity of his reaction which undermines all his

22 · Summaries

claims to moral authority, but he cannot resist it. Although we do not see it, presumably he gives orders to postpone Claudio's execution.

doom:	sentence
there's the vein:	that's the way
were forfeit once:	Adam's fall exposed man to sin and death until Christ came into the world to redeem him
the top of judgment:	God, the highest judge
Like man new made:	in the biblical account of the creation God breathed life into man's nostrils
glass:	crystal used in fortune telling
successive degrees:	subsequent development
Jove:	chief of the gods of classical antiquity
pelting:	insignificant
bolt:	thunderbolt
his glassy essence:	his true nature, either as it reflects God or as it is reflected in the mirror
spleens:	laughter was thought to originate in the spleen
weigh:	judge
skins the vice o'th'top:	covers the vice as new skin grows over a wound
breeds:	is stirred into life
sickles:	shekels, coins
preserved:	set apart from the world
virtuous season:	warm weather which gives life to the flower (Isabella) but corrupts the carrion (Angelo)
fond:	infatuated

Act II Scene 3

The Duke visits the prison where he meets Juliet and hears of Claudio's impending execution. Disguised as a friar, he learns that she is genuinely repentant for her sin and not just sorry because she has been found out. He tells her her lover must die the next day.

NOTES AND GLOSSARY:
This is the only scene where Juliet speaks. We see that she loves Claudio and recognises that his situation is as much her fault as his. The Duke's insistence that as the woman she is more to blame sounds rather harsh but would be common at that date. Juliet, like Claudio, seems refreshingly normal when compared with some of the play's moral extremists. The Duke's use of his disguise to discover his subjects' innermost thoughts both here and later may trouble some readers, but clearly his motives are good.

flaws: bursts of passion
blister'd her report: marred her reputation

Act II Scene 4

Angelo is attempting, unsuccessfully, to pray for help against temptation, when Isabella arrives. This time they are alone as they return to their discussion of the previous day. In Heaven's eyes, Angelo argues, Claudio has broken the moral law just as surely as if he had committed murder. But on earth, Isabella answers, we recognise some offences as more serious than others. He accepts her point, but turns it against her:

> Might there not be a charity in sin
> To save this brother's life? (lines 63–4)

Such a deed would be no sin at all, Isabella agrees, only to find that the sin he has in mind is not his own in bending the law to free Claudio, but her sin in offering her virginity to Angelo in exchange for her brother's life. In that case it is better that he should die, Isabella answers. Then is she not as cruel as the law itself, counters Angelo. She protests that there is no comparison between what she is asking of him and what he is asking of her. Surely he cannot be serious, but is simply testing her virtue? Angelo destroys her last hope, all 'seeming' (line 149) is over. He is now openly revealed as the would-be seducer, and Isabella as the outraged woman who threatens to blackmail him. Unless he pardons her brother she will expose him. No one will believe her, he answers, and unless she submits, Claudio will not only die, but die slowly and painfully.

Isabella can only hope that her brother will see things as she does and welcome death rather than her dishonour.

NOTES AND GLOSSARY:
This is the pivotal scene of the play, where 'blood', the underlying reality of emotion and desire, proves stronger than 'false seeming' (line 15), the modest outward appearance of both Angelo and Isabella. In his opening soliloquy Angelo reveals that the gravity on which he has prided himself is an empty show:

> Let's write good angel on the devil's horn –
> 'Tis not the devil's crest. (lines 16–17)

In spite of his name the devil has a part in Angelo's nature too, and it seems the larger part.

Once Isabella has abandoned a simple view of right and wrong she finds it difficult to be consistent. When Angelo argues that if she submits to him her soul will not be in danger since 'compell'd sins' (line 57) do not really count he is introducing a traditional moral talking-point, raised also in Shakespeare's own early poem *The Rape of Lucrece*.

Lucretia, the Roman lady raped by the emperor Tarquin, who killed herself rather than live on dishonoured, could be seen as either a model of heroic virtue or an example of spiritual pride. When Isabella declares 'I had rather give my body than my soul' (line 56), she is certainly sincere, but it is the physical aspect of what Angelo demands which offends her. Her final refusal in the most memorable line in the play, 'More than our brother is our chastity' (line 184), must shock us, and must have shocked audiences even at a time when female chastity was highly regarded and Shakespeare alters the words of the heroine in his source, substituting for 'honour' the word 'chastity' with its religious and sexual overtones. We may not agree with Isabella but we can sympathise with her dilemma. We see that she is not, as Lucio supposed, 'a thing enskied and sainted' (I.4.34), but a woman of flesh and blood.

It is sometimes suggested that Angelo's logic is impeccable as he turns the tables on her, but Isabella's answer holds good: 'lawful mercy/Is nothing kin to foul redemption' (lines 112–13). It is not his reasoning that defeats her, but her own confused emotions on the subject of sex. Angelo does not have right on his side, he simply has power, as his final words make clear: 'Say what you can: my false o'erweighs your true' (line 169).

invention: thought
sere: dry, withered
boot: advantage
for vain: uselessly
case: outer covering
habit: dress
swounds: faints
general subject: common people
coin heaven's image: beget illegitimate children
in restrained means: by unlawful methods
accompt: reckoning, account
nothing of your answer: nothing you need answer for
enciel'd shielded
gross: plainly
in the loss of question: for the sake of argument
die for ever: be damned eternally
of two houses: quite distinct
feodary: confederate
Owe and succeed thy weakness: possess and inherit the failing you mention
Men their creation mar: men violate their own god-given nature
credulous to: easily impressed by
destin'd livery: characteristic attributes of womanhood, in this case frailty

pluck on others: tempt others to expose themselves
I give my sensual race the rein: I let my sexual desires run free
prolixious: redundant
sufferance: suffering
make curtsey: bow
prompture: prompting

Act III Scene 1

The disguised Duke prepares Claudio for death which, he argues, will free him from all the troubles of life. Isabella arrives and the Duke leaves them together, but hides where he can hear their conversation. After some hesitation Isabella comes to the point:

If I would yield [Angelo] my virginity
Thou mightst be freed. (lines 97–8)

Unthinkable, he agrees, but then the reality of death becomes stronger than his moral scruples and he asks her to save him. Horrified to find her brother echoing Angelo's reasoning, she denounces his cowardice and storms out.

The Duke catches her as she leaves and asks her to wait for him. Meanwhile he tells Claudio that Angelo has merely been testing Isabella's virtue; even if she was willing she cannot help him, he must die, and, overcome by shame, Claudio now welcomes the idea.

Alone with Isabella the Duke reveals his plan. Mariana, once contracted to marry Angelo, but deserted by him when her dowry was lost, will take Isabella's place in his bed under cover of darkness: 'by this is your brother saved, your honour untainted, the poor Mariana advantaged, and the corrupt deputy scaled' (lines 253–6). Isabella agrees and leaves to accept Angelo's proposal while the Duke goes to prepare Mariana.

NOTES AND GLOSSARY:

The last scene has brought the action to a crisis; now the mechanism which will resolve it is revealed. One act of illicit sex, involving Claudio and Juliet, began it all, and another, involving Angelo and Mariana, will bring it to a conclusion. The play's irony depends on a series of similar parallels. In fact neither act is illicit, since both follow contracts to marry. Under Elizabethan law, Angelo's promise to marry can legally be broken as the dowry is unpaid, but if the couple sleep together then it is once more binding. This is what the Duke intends to bring about, but that Isabella should help him may lay her open to criticism.

If her own virginity is so precious, why should Mariana's be less so? In bringing Angelo and Mariana together is she not acting more like a bawd than a future nun? How can she escape the charge of hypocrisy in taking advantage of Mariana's situation?

First of all, since Mariana is willing and contracted to marry, the only person taken advantage of is Angelo, who is hardly in a position to take a high moral line. If Isabella has any doubts, she has the friar's word that 'the doubleness of the benefit defends the deceit from reproof' (lines 258-9). But in any case she is a changed woman from this point in the play, and after the outburst against her brother we do not hear again her earlier note of self-righteous indignation.

The Duke's opening speech, the longest in the play, is in the medieval tradition of the 'consolation' which helped the good Christian to die well, and uses familiar arguments. What is surprising, given his disguise, is that the Christian hope of an afterlife is not among the comforts he offers. Instead he defines death as the absence of the pains and uncertainties of the living. Claudio's own reply, after the Duke has left, 'Ay, but to die, and go we know not where' (line 117), stresses the presence of death as a physical fact and the uncertainty of what comes after death in lines which remind us of Hamlet's most famous soliloquy. Hamlet is not usually seen as a coward, and Claudio's weakness is one we can understand and excuse. When the Duke assures him he must die, his courage returns.

Isabella's ready sympathy for Mariana and her submissiveness to the friar mean that the scene ends with our thinking better of her than we did during her attack on her brother.

absolute: resolved
skyey influences: the stars were believed to influence human behaviour
accommodations: endowments
worm: snake, whose forked tongue was believed to sting
complexion: temperament
bowels: children
serpigo: a skin disease
palsied eld: feeble old age
moe: more
leiger: ambassador
appointment: preparation
durance: imprisonment
vastidity: vastness
determined scope: fixed limit
enew: put down
cast: cleared out
So to offend him still: freedom to go on offending
force: enforce

perdurably fin'd:	punished eternally
viewless:	invisible
shield:	forbid
my habit:	the friar's gown
resolve:	explain
discover:	expose
solemnity:	marriage ceremony
sinew:	substance
pretending:	alleging
frame:	prepare
holding up:	sustaining

Act III Scene 2

The Duke meets Elbow taking Pompey to prison; it seems he has not heeded Escalus's warning. Lucio enters and Pompey appeals to him for bail, but is refused. Left together Lucio and the supposed friar talk of Angelo's severity which Lucio contrasts with the absent Duke's leniency. The Duke's own transgressions made him tolerant of others; Lucio claims: 'he knew the service; and that instructed him to mercy' (lines 116–17). Because of his disguise, the Duke has to stand by and hear himself insulted as a lecher and 'a very superficial, ignorant, unweighing fellow' (line 136). He asks Lucio for his name and says he will ask him to repeat his accusations when the Duke returns. Lucio goes off, leaving him to reflect that no virtue is safe from slander.

Escalus and the Provost lead in Mistress Overdone, like Pompey bound for prison. She blames Lucio for her arrest, and reveals that she has been looking after his illegitimate child by Mistress Kate Keepdown, one of her prostitutes. Escalus asks that Lucio be sent for and that Claudio be attended by a priest before his death the next day. He is told that he has already been visited by the friar, and they talk of Claudio and the Duke himself, who according to Escalus was a 'gentleman of all temperance' (line 231) who aimed above all at self-knowledge. Escalus regrets Angelo's severity and is told that such firmness is a virtue provided that his own behaviour measures up to the same strict standards. Left alone, the Duke reflects on Angelo's duplicity and rehearses his plan to defeat him.

NOTES AND GLOSSARY:
Editors have usually divided the act here, although in the First Folio there is no scene division.

Lucio's conversation with Pompey contrasts with his meeting with Claudio in Act I Scene 2. Obviously Claudio was more deserving of his help, but Lucio's refusal here should prevent us from sentimentalising him. There is no evidence for Mistress Overdone's belief that Lucio has denounced her, but he has broken his promise to marry Mistress Kate. His action here provides an ironic parallel with Angelo's desertion of Mariana, and Mistress Overdone's care for the child shows that whatever her vices she is not unkind. She is kinder, no doubt, than Angelo, who provides for Juliet's child only because the law requires it.

The scene is interesting mainly for the light it throws on the Duke. His denunciation of Pompey's 'filthy vice' (line 22) is quite unlike Escalus's good-humoured sternness. Perhaps his friar's gown has something to do with it. We have some difficulty in arriving at a personal judgement of the Duke because his words often have a generalised, sententious weight about them, seen at the very end of the scene where prose gives way to a moralising poem:

> He who the sword of heaven will bear
> Should be as holy as severe: (lines 254-5)

All that the Duke claims for himself is that he is 'a scholar, a statesman, and a soldier' (line 143), a modest enough description. He would be less than human if he was not irritated by Lucio's accusations. There is a similar scene in *Henry V* before the battle of Agincourt when the King in disguise argues with one of his soldiers.

It is sometimes suggested that Lucio knows he is talking to the Duke. He mentions his 'usurp(ing) the beggary he was never born to' (line 90) although it is generally believed that the Duke has gone to Poland. But if he had recognised the Duke he would never dare talk as he does. That he is unknowingly so near the mark adds to the audience's amusement.

Perhaps because we have reservations about the Duke's spying on others we are not too sorry to see him made uncomfortable as a result. He must be reassured by Escalus's good opinion, since what he has seen earlier has justified his fears for the moral health of the city. There is a 'fever on goodness' (line 221) which may prove fatal.

bastard: a Spanish wine, also the illegitimate children resulting from Pompey's trade
two usuries: lechery and money-lending
your waist: the cord around the friar's waist is not unlike the hangman's rope
Pygmalion's images: statues which in the classical myth the sculptor brought to life, but here meaning prostitutes, Pompey's creations
trot: old woman
powdered: beef was salted or 'powdered' in a tub, but a treatment for venereal disease also involved fumigation in a sweating-tub

unshunned:	unavoidable
keep the house:	look after the house, and also stay indoors (inevitable in the prison)
motion:	puppet
codpiece:	covering for the male genitals, also the genitals themselves
clack-dish:	begging bowl
inward:	intimate acquaintance
I prithee:	I ask you
greater file:	majority
tun-dish:	funnel
ungenitured:	sexless
untrussing:	unfastening his hose
mutton on Fridays:	good Catholics fasted on Fridays, but mutton also meant prostitutes
come Philip and Jacob:	on 1 May, the festival of St Philip and St James
entertainment:	reception
shore:	limit

Act IV Scene 1

Mariana is listening to a love-song when the Duke enters, still in his disguise as a friar. Isabella arrives and Mariana leaves them for a moment while he learns of the arrangements for the assignation with Angelo that night. Isabella then goes out to explain them to Mariana. The Duke again reflects on the false report to which authority, 'place and greatness' (line 60), is always subject, until the two girls return. Mariana has agreed to take Isabella's place and the Duke reassures her that since Angelo is her contracted husband 'to bring you thus together 'tis no sin' (line 73).

NOTES AND GLOSSARY:

The song is best known in a setting by John Wilson, but as he was still a child in 1604 some other tune must have been used for the early performances. The Duke's speech at line 60 seems to have little to do with the business in hand and it has been suggested that the lines have been taken from his soliloquy in the previous scene (lines 179–83) to give him something to say while Isabella reveals the plan to Mariana.

planched:	made of planks
In action all of precept:	by spoken directions rather than actual demonstration
'greed:	agreed
a repair:	to go
flourish:	embellish
tithe's:	corn to pay tithes or taxes

30 · Summaries

Act IV Scene 2

The Provost offers Pompey his freedom if he will act as assistant executioner. After some banter with Abhorson, who thinks a bawd not good enough to assist him, Pompey accepts. Claudio and Barnardine are called to be Pompey's first customers, and Claudio appears briefly, but Barnardine is asleep. The Duke arrives with hopes of a pardon for Claudio, but when a messenger follows him it is with an order for the execution to go ahead even earlier than planned. To prevent this the Duke suggests that Barnardine be beheaded in Claudio's place, and after some hesitation the Provost agrees. In his disguise as friar the Duke goes out to hear Barnardine's confession.

NOTES AND GLOSSARY:
The job of executioner was not a popular one, though Abhorson takes pride in it as a 'mystery', a skilled trade. His reasons for doing so are a mystery in the other sense of the word, as the text is obscure at this point and it is not easy to follow the argument about clothing (traditionally the condemned man's clothes went to the executioner). The unholy alliance of Pompey and Abhorson shows that justice in one of its aspects is little different from vice: as the Provost tells them 'you weigh equally: a feather will turn the scale' (line 28).

As the Duke has not foreseen that Angelo will break his promise to Isabella, he has to improvise a solution. Since Barnardine is to be executed later the same day he provides the obvious answer.

sirrah: fellow
snatches: plays on words
gyves: fetters
yare: adroit
meal'd: mixed or stained
unsisting postern: unyielding door
siege: seat
putting-on: incitement
desperately mortal: without hope of immortality
manifested effect: clear demonstration
th'unfolding star: the first star, which signals to the shepherd to let the sheep out of the fold

Act IV Scene 3

Pompey reflects that his new occupation is no great change since most of his former customers are here in prison. Barnardine is brought out in accordance with the Duke's new arrangement. The disguised Duke offers to pray with the condemned man but Barnardine, half drunk, refuses. The Duke is unwilling that even a murderer should die unconfessed, but luckily another prisoner, Ragozine, has died that morning and the Provost suggests that his head should go to Angelo in place of Claudio's. Barnardine and Claudio are to be hidden until the Duke's return and the Provost is to take letters to Angelo asking him to meet the Duke outside the city where his re-entry is to be made public.

Isabella arrives, expecting to hear of her brother's release, and the Duke decides to tell her that he is already dead. Her first thoughts are of revenge, but he advises her to take her case to the Duke on his return the following day. She is to take a letter to Friar Peter asking him to Mariana's house where he will learn of the relevant details so that he can support their case against Angelo. Lucio enters, condoles with Isabella, and resumes his argument with the supposed friar about the 'old fantastical duke of dark corners' (line 156). This time we hear that Lucio is the father of Kate Keepdown's child, though when brought before the Duke for the offence he had denied it on oath.

NOTES AND GLOSSARY:
The introduction of Ragozine as a further substitute for Claudio may seem an unnecessary complication, but it shows the Duke's humanity, and prevents the comedy being marred with bloodshed.

In strictly realistic terms the Duke's decision to let Isabella believe her brother dead would be hard to defend, but it is a necessary stage in her moral re-education, to be completed in the final act. In Shakespeare's *King Lear* the disguised Edgar delays revealing his identity to his blinded father for similar reasons.

Lucio's sympathy is more spontaneous, and no doubt he did love Claudio as he says, but his thoughts soon turn elsewhere.

peaches: denounces as
'for the Lord's sake': with these words the prisoners begged from passers-by
clap-into: hurry to
ghostly: spiritual
ward: part of the prison
unmeet: unsuitable
holds: cells
journal: daily
By cold gradation: coldly, step by step
bosom: heart's desire
combined: bound
fain: compelled
for my head: to save my head

set me to't: arouse me to sexual desire
beholding: indebted
woodman: huntsman (of women)
medlar: a fruit, also a prostitute

Act IV Scene 4

Angelo and Escalus are puzzled by letters received from the Duke, who has asked for his arrival to be announced. If anyone has any complaint or request he will deal with it in public. Left alone, Angelo is alarmed by this news, but trusts that Isabella's modesty will keep her quiet. If not, his own reputation should protect him. He ordered Claudio's death in case he should try to revenge his sister's violation, but now half regrets that he broke his word.

NOTES AND GLOSSARY:
Angelo begins to feel remorse and reflects that once the path of virtue is lost 'nothing goes right' (line 32). His confusion now contrasts with his cold confidence before: 'we would, and we would not' (line 32). We may remember that at their first meeting it was Isabella who was 'at war 'twixt will and will not' (II.2.33).

disvouched: contradicted
devices: plots, contrivances
Betimes: early
men of sort and suit: men of rank with a retinue of followers
unpregnant: incapable
tongue: accuse
credent bulk: massive credibility
sense: feeling, passion

Act IV Scene 5

The Duke, no longer in disguise, sends Friar Peter to make final arrangements for his return. Varrius enters and accompanies the Duke on his way.

NOTES AND GLOSSARY:
Varrius is presumably one of the unnamed lords in the opening scene. It has been suggested that his name points to another of Shakespeare's sources for the Duke. Varius was the father of Severus (208–35), a Roman emperor celebrated for reforming the morals of his time.

blench: deviate

Act IV Scene 6

Isabella and Mariana discuss the stories they are going to tell. Isabella would like to reveal the whole truth, but the disguised Duke has evidently asked her to make no mention of Mariana's part in the affair. Mariana herself will confront Angelo with his offence to her. They have been warned that the evidence may seem to go against them. Friar Peter comes in to take them to a place from which they can approach the Duke, who is to arrive at any moment.

NOTES AND GLOSSARY:
Isabella's willingness to depart from the strict truth when the cause is good is evidence of a change in her. She is still reluctant, but submits to the direction of those she trusts.

physic: medicine
hent: taken their places at

Act V Scene 1

After the Duke has been welcomed by Angelo and Escalus, Isabella comes forward to ask for justice. The Duke refers her to Angelo while she tries to explain that he is the last person to whom she would turn. Angelo intervenes to say that she is deranged, and the Duke, hearing the violence of her denunciation, seems inclined to agree with him, but he lets her speak. She begins her story, Lucio interrupting to confirm his part in taking her to Angelo. He repeatedly interferes, to the Duke's mounting irritation, as the scene continues. The Duke objects to the improbability of her account of Angelo:

> If he has so offended,
> He would have weigh'd thy brother by himself,
> And not have cut him off. (lines 113-15)

She is taken out to prison, asking for Friar Lodowick. This was the name the Duke had adopted while in disguise, and he now asks for any news of the friar. Lucio remembers him as 'a very scurvy fellow' (line 139) he met at the prison the previous night. Friar Peter says that Lodowick is sick and that he has come in his place with evidence and a witness to defend Angelo. The witness is Mariana, veiled; she explains that on the night when Isabella claims that she went to Angelo's lodgings he was in bed with her. He is in fact her husband, and she unveils to reveal herself. Still Angelo denies that he has had any recent contact with her and declares that the two women have been set on to slander him by some third party. He asks to be allowed to investigate the matter, and Friar Lodowick is sent for, while the Duke himself withdraws for a time.

34 · Summaries

Isabella is brought back, and the Provost returns with the Duke in his disguise as Friar Lodowick. When questioned he complains about the Duke's injustice in leaving Angelo, the accused, to hear Isabella's case. He goes on to denounce the corruption of the city. Lucio again intervenes to say that this is indeed the friar he spoke of, and that he called the Duke a 'fleshmonger, a fool, and a coward' (lines 331–2). The supposed friar protests, 'I love the Duke as I love myself' (line 339), but Angelo, Escalus and Lucio all turn on him, and Lucio pulls the friar's hood from his head.

Revealed at last, the Duke takes charge and asks Angelo if he has anything to say. Overcome with guilt, he asks only for immediate execution. He admits he was contracted to Mariana and is taken out to marry her. While they are gone the Duke explains to Isabella that he would have saved her brother if Angelo had not acted so quickly. Angelo returns to hear his sentence:

> An Angelo for Claudio; death for death.
> Haste still pays haste, and leisure answers leisure;
> Like doth quit like, and Measure still for Measure. (lines 407–9)

Mariana begs for mercy for her new husband and asks Isabella to support her. Isabella kneels to the Duke. She admits that her beauty may be partly to blame for corrupting Angelo's former virtue, and since her chastity is still intact in spite of his attempts, and since her brother's life was legally taken, she asks that he be spared.

The Duke is unpersuaded but turns to another offence, asking why Claudio was executed before the appointed time without a special warrant. The Provost explains that he was reluctant to carry out his instructions and at least saved another prisoner whose death had been ordered. Barnardine is brought in and pardoned by the Duke, though Friar Peter is asked to help him to a better state of mind. The Provost then brings forward another prisoner 'who should have died when Claudio lost his head' (line 486) and Claudio himself is revealed.

The Duke pardons him, and asks Isabella for her hand in marriage. Angelo too is pardoned, but Lucio is condemned to marry Mistress Kate, then to be whipped and hanged. Immediately, though, the Duke relents; the marriage is to be his only punishment. Lucio protests, but the Duke moves on into his final speech. Claudio and Angelo are told to look after their wives, Escalus and the Provost are thanked for their loyalty, and all are led out to the Duke's palace.

NOTES AND GLOSSARY:

This is a crowded scene, though most of the action involves the completion of mechanism already set in motion in earlier acts. The Duke repeatedly attempts to prick Angelo's conscience, making him the judge of his own cause, yet Angelo remains obdurate, even when the two girls seem likely to go to prison. This is necessary if the twists and turns of the plot are not to be short-circuited, but makes it still more difficult for the audience to sympathise with him.

Isabella's distress when her story is not believed is part of the moral pressure applied to Angelo, apparently without success, but may also be a further chastening for her attack on Claudio in Act III. Mariana, who is Shakespeare's addition to the story, adds to the pressure and also makes Angelo guilty of the act for which he condemned Claudio. We enjoy the ingenuity of the plotting here, noticing that Angelo's 'alibi' against Isabella's accusation involves admitting his relationship with Mariana, though for the moment he denies both.

The Duke's return to his former diatribes against the depravity of his city, though it brings out Escalus's loyalty to his master, perhaps disturbs us. Corruption on this scale seems beyond the power of comedy to cure, but the Duke is speaking in his guise of friar, and his eye is on Angelo.

Angelo's confession, when at last it comes, is complete; his answer to Escalus's pained reproof shows him in a new light: 'I am sorry that such sorrow I procure' (line 472). Mariana's plea for his life is purely disinterested, since the Duke has explained that Angelo's death would leave her a wealthy widow.

Isabella's decision to ask for mercy for the man she thinks responsible for the death of her brother reverses her earlier attitude towards Claudio himself:

I'll pray a thousand prayers for thy death;
No word to save thee. (III.1.145–6)

In Giraldi Cinthio's version of the story (see p. 36), the heroine pardons the judge only after her brother is seen to be alive. Shakespeare reverses the order to underline the change in Isabella.

Barnardine's usefulness has been lessened by the availability of Ragozine's head, but his pardon again illustrates the Duke's mercy, which extends not only to those in love with life, like Claudio, but to those 'insensible to mortality' (IV.2.142–3).

Lucio's presence has added a note of comedy to what might have been a rather mechanical apportionment of rewards and punishments. The Duke is often criticised for his harshness to his detractor, but in the scheme of the play his punishment parallels Angelo's, and is in any case nothing worse than marriage to the mother of his own child. That the Duke should marry Isabella seems equally fitting, since we have seen that the convent is not for her. He embodies those qualities of wisdom and temperance which in the light of her experience seem most worthy of respect and most likely to bring happiness.

cousin:	fellow nobleman
bonds:	obligations
vail your regard:	look down
conjure:	appeal to
caracts:	insignia
inequality:	injustice or incongruity
to the matter:	appropriate
refell'd:	refused
concupiscible:	sensual
proper:	belonging
practice:	plot
swing'd:	thrashed
one ungot:	a man not yet born
convented:	summoned
punk:	prostitute
match:	appointment
proportions:	dowry
informal:	deranged
throughly:	thoroughly
Cucullus non facit monachum:	(*Latin*) 'the hood does not make the monk', things are not always what they seem
light:	unchaste
The Duke's in us:	we represent the Duke
touse:	tear
stew:	a dish of boiled meat, and also a brothel
like the forfeits in a barber's shop:	barbers acted as surgeons and dentists, and the forfeits must refer to their bloody activities while so employed
As much in mock as mark:	less heeded than laughed at
fleshmonger:	fornicator
giglets:	harlots
sheep-biting:	wolfish
office:	service
passes:	actions
Advertising:	attentive
remonstrance:	revelation
brain'd:	destroyed
salt:	salacious
squar'st:	regulate
remission:	inclination to pardon
luxury:	lechery
trick:	custom
behind:	reserved for you
gratulate:	gratifying

Part 3
Commentary

The title

The title comes from the Bible, Saint Matthew's Gospel, Chapter 7, verses 1–5, where the whole context, that of Christ's Sermon on the Mount, is relevant to the themes of the play:

> Judge not, that ye be not judged. For with what judgment ye judge, ye shall be judged: and with what measure ye mete, it shall be measured to you again. And why beholdest thou the mote that is in thy brother's eye, but considerest not the beam that is in thine own eye... Thou hypocrite, first cast out the beam out of thine own eye; and then shalt thou see clearly to cast out the mote out of thy brother's eye.

The phrase, however, seems to have been used more generally to describe a harsh conception of justice as retribution, and it is in this sense that the Duke quotes it in Act V Scene 1:

> An Angelo for Claudio; death for death.
> Haste still pays haste, and leisure answers leisure;
> Like doth quit like, and Measure still for Measure. (lines 407–9)

Other versions of the story lay the emphasis here, asking the audience to admire and enjoy the way the punishment fits the crime, but Shakespeare chose to follow the spirit of Christ's teaching and to argue for temperance. In *A Mirror for Magistrates* (1574) we meet the same argument:

> 'The property of Temperance is to covet nothing which may be repented: not to exceed the bounds of measure, and to keep desire under the yoke of Reason.'

The sources

Shakespeare's usual method was to take a story from some other author but to adapt it freely to his needs, and *Measure for Measure* is no exception to this. In 1578 George Whetstone (*c.* 1551–87) had published a two-part play, *The Right Excellent and Famous History of Promos and Cassandra*, which gives the main lines of the plot as we have it in Shakespeare. Whetstone republished it as a short story in his *A*

Heptameron of Civil Discourses (1582). He himself seems to have read the tale in a collection of Italian stories by Giraldi Cinthio (1504–73), the *Hecatommithi*, published in 1565, and he may conceivably have known the play, *Epitia,* which Cinthio made from the story some time before his death in 1573. Since Cinthio's *Hecatommithi* is the only known source for the story of *Othello,* which Shakespeare must have been writing at about the same time as *Measure for Measure,* it seems very likely that he too knew the Italian version, or a French translation of it.

The story of the corrupt judge who will release the condemned man only in return for the 'monstrous ransom' of a woman's honour was well known, and there are other possible sources, or at least analogues, for the play. G. Bullough's *Narrative and Dramatic Sources of Shakespeare,* Volume II, prints some of them, and the New Arden edition of the play includes relevant extracts in an appendix. (See Part 5 of these notes for further details.)

Measure for Measure differs from Cinthio and Whetstone in elaborating the part played by the ruler, and in saving the heroine's honour. In the other versions there is no Mariana to take her place, though this substitution, the 'bed-trick', is another Italian borrowing, and Shakespeare had himself recently used it in *All's Well that Ends Well.* As a result, the wise ruler can only resolve the situation by marrying the wronged woman to the man who has violated her. Shakespeare clearly thought he could do better than that.

Critical history

We know nothing of how the first audiences received the play, though they at least saw it as Shakespeare intended. In the following years it became fashionable to 'improve' the text, and in 1661 Sir William Davenant (1606–68) even combined it with *Much Ado About Nothing* to produce his own *The Law Against Lovers.* As Shakespeare's reputation grew this kind of cannibalism was no longer tolerated, although cuts would still be made to the 'indecent' parts of the play. *Measure for Measure* survived all this, and famous actresses such as Mrs Cibber and Sarah Siddons (1755–1831) had great success as Isabella.

Some of the earliest critics had the same difficulties we have today. In 1753 Charlotte Lennox (1720–1804) was troubled both by the form and by the morality of the play:

> Shakespear made a wrong Choice of his Subject, since he was resolved to torture it into a Comedy ... this play therefore being absolutely Defective in a due Distribution of Rewards and Punishments.
> (*Shakespear Illustrated,* 1753–5)

Dr Johnson (1709–84), with his understanding of Shakespeare's 'mingled drama' as neither comedy nor tragedy but 'exhibiting the real state of sublunary nature', was less puzzled by the form, but he too was worried by the ending:

> Angelo's crimes were such, as must sufficiently justify punishment, whether its end be to secure the innocent from wrong, or to deter guilt by example; and I believe every reader feels some indignation when he finds him spared. (*Notes on Shakespeare*, 1765)

Fifty years later the reactions of S. T. Coleridge (1772–1834) were much more violent:

> It is a hateful work, although Shakespearean throughout. Our feelings of justice are grossly wounded in Angelo's escape. Isabella herself contrives to be unamiable, and Claudio is detestable.
> (*Table Talk*, 1888)

His contemporary, William Hazlitt (1778–1830), found more to recommend the play though he too thought the subject unpleasing: 'there is in general a want of passion; the affections are at a stand; our sympathies are repulsed and defeated in all directions' (*Characters of Shakespeare's Plays*, 1817). Yet he takes a step away from the earlier notion of the morality of a work as the 'due Distribution of Rewards and Punishments' when he comes to examine Barnardine:

> Shakespeare was in one sense the least moral of writers; for morality (commonly so called) is made up of antipathies; and his talent consisted in sympathy with human nature, in all its shapes, degrees, depressions, and elevations (*Characters of Shakespeare's Plays*, 1817).

Walter Pater (1839–94) developed this view of justice and morality in a still more subtle account of the play:

> It is for this finer justice, a justice based on a more delicate appreciation of the true conditions of men and things, a true respect of persons in our estimate of actions, that the people in *Measure for Measure* cry out as they pass before us; and as the poetry of this play is full of the peculiarities of Shakespeare's poetry, so in its ethics it is an epitome of Shakespeare's moral judgments. (*Appreciations*, 1889)

Not all readers were persuaded to this opinion, although Victorian piety often admired the purity of Isabella's moral character where Dr Johnson had rather cynically questioned her forgiveness of Angelo:

> I am afraid our varlet poet intended to inculcate that woman think ill of nothing that raises the credit of their beauty, and are ready, however virtuous, to pardon any act which they think incited by their own charm. (*Notes on Shakespeare*, 1765)

Objections to the ending were still heard, Algernon Swinburne (1837–1909) repeating Coleridge's feeling that it 'baffles the strong indignant claim of justice'.

Moving into the present century we find the problematic nature of the play generally accepted, and often connected with some supposed disturbance in Shakespeare's private life. This was challenged in the single most influential essay on the play, G. Wilson Knight's chapter on 'Measure for Measure and the Gospels' in his book *The Wheel of Fire*,* where he argued that 'the poetic atmosphere is one of religion and critical morality ... the simplest way to focus correctly the quality and unity of *Measure for Measure* is to read it on the analogy of Jesus' parables'. Armed with this key he found the ending 'exquisite ... no play of Shakespeare shows more deliberate purpose, more consummate skill in structural technique, and, finally, more penetrating ethical and psychological insight'. Where Wilson Knight saw analogies with the Gospels, other critics have seen deliberate allegory. Roy Battenhouse** identifies the characters of the play with figures from Christian myth, the Duke acting as the God who comes to earth to lead his people to grace and justice. Still others have restated Wilson Knight's understanding of the subtlety and coherence of the play in secular terms, notably F. R. Leavis in an essay on 'The Greatness of *Measure for Measure*'.†

A willingness to see poetic drama as less narrowly bound by the rules of psychological realism helped to win favour for the play, though the difficulties experienced over the years were still present to many readers. Perhaps because of the difficulties, the play continues to arouse strong feelings and divided opinions, effects which have made it popular in the theatre in recent times.

The characters

We generally think of plays as involving a group of characters, and of plot as 'character in action', to be examined with all the psychological understanding of which we are capable. This critical tradition culminated in A. C. Bradley (1851–1935)'s fine book *Shakespearean Tragedy* (1904), but nearer our own time Bradley's concentration on character has been questioned. Our relationship with characters in plays, we are told, cannot be like our contact with people in the world outside. Even Shakespeare failed when he tried to separate the characters from the plays; Sir John Falstaff, when he was revived for *The*

---

*G. Wilson Knight, *The Wheel of Fire*, Oxford University Press, London, 1930.
**Roy Battenhouse, '*Measure for Measure*' and Christian Doctrine of the Atonement' P.M.L.A., 61, 1949.
†F. R. Leavis, 'The Greatness of *Measure for Measure*' *Scrutiny*, 10, 1942; reprinted in *The Common Pursuit*, Chatto and Windus, London 1952.

Merry Wives of Windsor, was only a pale shadow of the substantial man he had been in *Henry IV*, because that substance had been part of a whole context of feelings and ideas expressed in the texture of the play as much as in the individual characters. The same caution is necessary when approaching *Measure for Measure*, where the characters are subservient to the plot and judged by the standards of real life can be found guilty of all kinds of inhumanity and inconsistency. Yet the plays do hold the mirror up to nature, as Dr Johnson believed:

> His persons act and speak by the influence of those general passions and principles by which all minds are agitated, and the whole system of life is continued in motion. (*Preface to Shakespeare*, 1765)

The Duke

His part is easily the longest; he has the first word and the last. Shakespeare greatly extends the role as he found it in his source, and involves him in all the crucial developments of the plot. In Whetstone, for example, the condemned brother only escapes because his gaoler takes pity on him. In making his changes Shakespeare risks reducing the other characters to puppets who act only at the Duke's bidding. It is true that the Duke is responsible for the turning-point of the action when he suggests the substitution of Mariana for Isabella, but in general he acts as a safety-net rather than a puppet-master. In putting on the friar's gown he abandons something of the power he enjoys as Duke, and has to rely on persuasion and advice. Even the Provost is not simply ordered to postpone the executions. The Duke introduces Mariana, but he leaves Isabella to persuade her to play her part. Although he intends to save Claudio's life, he does not reveal what he has arranged, and Claudio reacts as though he was indeed to die. The final scene is stagemanaged by the Duke, but he continues to act passively, leaving Angelo to condemn himself and the women to argue their case. Angelo's pardon comes only when Isabella adds her voice to Mariana's to ask for his life, still believing that the Duke has been too late to save her brother. Even the Duke's unmasking is curiously contrived, so that it is Lucio who restores him to his rightful role.

Throughout the Duke leaves his subjects free to act as their natures dictate, intervening only when necessary to prevent comedy turning to tragedy. This intervention becomes increasingly necessary in the second half of the play and is the source of most of the objections to the ending, but it seems implicit in Shakespeare's conception from the beginning. It has been claimed that the play collapses after Act III Scene 1, when we have seen 'what our seemers be' (I.3.54) and are left to spend the last two acts watching the Duke rescue the situation against all plausibility.

Yet the Duke's role is essentially educative, and by that stage the education of Isabella, Angelo and Claudio has scarcely begun.

In talking about the Duke we are inevitably led to talk about the other characters, and this illustrates one of the difficulties of the role. Since he remains above and beyond the pressures which make for dramatic excitement he has only a limited interest for us. In a later play of Shakespeare's, *The Tempest,* Prospero has some of the same characteristics, but the action is more closely bound up with his own experience. Shakespeare might have chosen to write a comedy about a Duke who 'contended especially to know himself' (III.2.226–7), but *Measure for Measure* is not that play.

When the first audiences heard the Duke announce his intention of remaining in Vienna in disguise, they would not ask 'What kind of man would do such a thing?' but would direct their attention forward, as invited, to see what would follow from the decision. They recognised the action as that of the wise ruler who wished to examine and improve the working of his state, an action familiar to them from other stories and carrying its own justification. Yet even as we recognise the convention, we notice the way Shakespeare enriches it. It seems the Duke has been at fault in letting slip the enforcement of the laws. True, we can dismiss this as an excuse to conceal the real reason for his actions, but it does not occur in Whetstone or Cinthio, and Shakespeare could easily have invented some other excuse which did not compromise his character. The Duke's warning against Angelo's cloistered virtue seems to reflect on his own love of 'the life remov'd' (I.3.8). He scorns 'the dribbling dart of love' (I.3.2), but, like Angelo, finds that he is less immune than he had imagined. Here at least his self-knowledge is incomplete. In the *Advancement of Learning* the following year Bacon was to write 'in this theatre of man's life it is reserved only for God and angels to be lookers-on'. The Duke is a man himself, and finds he too has a part to play, though not the main one.

We may think we understand the Duke's role, but for an actor there is still the problem of representing him on stage. We assume he is older than Angelo, but not too old to think of marrying Isabella. Temperamentally he seems fitted for the behind-the-scenes part which he plays throughout most of the play:

> I love the people,
> But do not like to stage me to their eyes (I.1.67–8)

The disguise of friar seems not only convenient but congenial, since his mode of life is austere, 'Rather rejoicing to see another merry, than merry at anything which professed to make him rejoice' (III.2.229–30). When at the beginning of Act III he counsels Claudio to accept death willingly, we feel that his own philosophy is represented, and significantly there are none of the references to a Christian afterlife which a friar might have added. Producers often seize on Lucio's phrase 'the old fantastical duke of dark corners' (IV.3.156) to create a cynically inscrutable character, but a sardonic tolerance, prone at times to blacker moods when he reflects on the corruption around him, would seem to be the keynote of the Duke's personality.

Angelo

Angelo recognises the irony of his own name (II.4.16–17) but it helps us to see the kind of character he is: as F. R. Leavis argues, not 'a certified criminal-type, capable of a wickedness that marks him off from you and me',* but a man with the potential for something better. The high opinion that Escalus and the Duke have of him must be based on something more than his sexual abstinence. We are to believe with Isabella that 'a due sincerity govern'd his deed/Till he did look on me' (V.1.444–5) Certainly he is sincere when he says that he is willing to be judged by the same severe laws he applies to others. It is not that he thinks he is without faults, but that he is confident of his power to keep the faults in check. As Lucio says 'he doth rebate and blunt his natural edge/With profits of the mind, study and fast' (I.4.60–1). When he looks on Isabella his defences prove inadequate. True, his earlier integrity has been of a narrow and unsympathetic kind, based on an ignorance of the value of emotion, and since he is accustomed to think of sexual impulses as shameful, when he feels them towards Isabella he can only despise himself. He is honest enough to see that she is virtuous, so his feelings separate them still further, and there can be no mutuality of love. She is the 'flower' and he the 'carrion' (II.2.67). Since his whole legalistic way of thinking makes it impossible for him to recognise degrees of sinfulness, when he falls he falls completely. He refuses to present his actions either to Isabella or to himself as less wicked than he knows them to be. In so far as he is a villian, he is much closer to Shakespeare's Macbeth than to his Iago.

But, it may be objected, what about his treatment of Mariana? Surely this shows him as a hypocrite from first to last? It is tempting to argue that the offences to Isabella and Mariana belong to separate moral accounts, and that the desertion of Mariana is essential to the plot; she must be available to take Isabella's place. Certainly the offences are different in kind, the attempt on Isabella the result of passion while Mariana's desertion depends on the coldness which distinguishes the earlier Angelo; he is 'a marble to her tears' (III.1.229). He behaved badly, but perhaps not unforgivably. Even his excuse for breaking off the match, that 'her reputation was disvalu'd/In levity' (V.1.221–2),

*F. R. Leavis, *The Common Pursuit*, 1952, p. 171

might be the result of his own much-prized 'gravity' which would see normal human emotion as suspect.

His repentance is complete, and a good actor can add something to the few words Shakespeare provides for his contrition. We can never like him, and will probably feel that Mariana is much too good for him, but if she can forgive him, why should not we?

Isabella

Isabella's vocation as a nun is not found in the sources, but it is central to Shakespeare's conception of her character. Her first words show her 'wishing a more strict restraint' (I.4.4) with a novice's enthusiasm. Lucio's half-serious view of her as a 'thing enskied and sainted' (I.4.34) recognises her sincerity but also draws attention to her connection through her womanhood with a world outside the convent gates. In her first interview with Angelo she has the moral authority to carry the argument of the play in appealing for Christian mercy, but her attack on the pride that stems from ignorance though directed at him will rebound on herself. When she goes out she is almost sure her case is won; in return she will offer Angelo 'prayers from preserved souls . . . whose minds are dedicate/To nothing temporal' (II.2.154–6). This is the retreat which Angelo denies her at their second meeting; he wants not her prayers but her body.

At first her reactions are conventional enough: 'I had rather give my body than my soul' (II.4.56). But her revulsion grows, and soon she will die, as she says, rather than 'yield/My body up to shame' (II.4.104–5). We sympathise with her anger, even while we are disturbed by its violence and the course it takes, until her final words pull us up short:

> Then, Isabel live chaste, and brother, die:
> More than our brother is our chastity. (II.4.183–4)

It is in the next scene that she becomes most like Angelo, 'blood' blotting out all regard for other people. Claudio's request that she should sin to save a brother's life, made when death is the only alternative, cannot be morally equated with Angelo's proposal, yet she turns all her anger on him: 'I'll pray a thousand prayers for thy death;/No word to save thee' (III.1.145–6).

So far it is generally agreed that Isabella's character is powerful and convincing, so powerful it is often said, that her behaviour in the rest of the play is quite inconsistent. Yet, once her anger has cooled, the problem still remains; she is not to be allowed the luxury of martyrdom, but must work to repair the situation through means which she may find uncongenial. The Duke will school her in her duties and Mariana will give her lessons in generosity. The final act will chasten her still further when she has to adopt the character of deflowered maid which she has refused in reality. No doubt the picture of womanhood to which she is asked to conform requires some effort of historical imagination, but Shakespeare has no use for her militancy.

Though she is not given much to say, her forgiveness of Angelo is a crucial point of the play, and it is strange that one critic should argue that 'not having become Angelo's wife (as in the sources), she has no reason to recommend him to mercy as well as to justice'.* The reason is provided by the whole meaning of the play, and it fits her to accept the Duke's offer of marriage. This, we take it, is what does happen, though Shakespeare does not give us her answer.

Claudio

Claudio's 'cowardice' has often troubled the critics, though it is expressed in the finest speech in the play (III.1.117-31). William Empson thinks that the very minor part he has in the final scene, where Whetstone's Andrugio had acted generously to save the judge now married to his sister, is evidence that Shakespeare found 'the behaviour of Claudio disgusting'†. Claudio's words when we first meet him in conversation with Lucio make it clear that he sees himself at fault. There is no extravagant bitterness, and he impresses us more favourably than he would if he simply denied any blame and complained of his hard luck. His love for Juliet strikes us as genuine, and at that date the delay over her dowry would not suggest that he was unduly mercenary.

When we see him in the death cell he is calm and composed. His reason is satisfied with the friar's arguments, but when the reality of death comes home to him his youth resists it as inevitably as Isabella's chastity resists Angelo's embrace:

To lie in cold obstruction, and to rot;
This sensible warm motion to become
A kneaded clod ... 'tis too horrible. (III.1.118, 127)

The weakness is momentary, and he asks Isabella's pardon when she is at last persuaded to listen. Unless we are sure that in the same circumstances we should behave differently, we are in no position to despise him.

Lucio

Lucio is Shakespeare's invention throughout, useful in many small ways for the working of the plot, and a necessary source of humour in a comedy where the central characters never laugh. Like many

*E.M.W. Tillyard, *Shakespeare's Problem Plays*, Chatto, London, 1957, p. 132
†W. Empson, *The Structure of Complex Words*, Chatto, London, 1951, p. 280.

comparable figures in Shakespeare's comedies, Parolles in the recently completed *All's Well that Ends Well* or Falstaff in the newly revived *The Merry Wives of Windsor,* he is amoral rather than immoral, so that our view of him constantly changes. When we first meet him his jokes with the two gentlemen associate sexuality with venereal disease, but two scenes later the sexuality of Claudio and Juliet, as he reports it to Isabella, becomes 'as blossoming time/That from the seedness the bare fallow brings/To teeming foison' (I.4.41–3). His readiness to help Claudio contrasts with his unconcern for Pompey. His presence at the interview between Isabella and Angelo helps us to see that the debate of abstract principles is also a battle between the sexes. He lends the warmth which Isabella's cold rectitude lacks. Although his comments deflate the moral pretentions of others, he himself has no hatred of the flesh, and he is never cynically destructive as is Thersites in Shakespeare's *Troilus and Cressida,* a play sometimes grouped with *Measure for Measure,* but quite different in tone and atmosphere.

He illustrates a general lawlessness less easily handled than the conventional vice of Pompey and Mistress Overdone, and it is significant that he singles out the disguised Duke, the embodiment of the law, for his attentions: 'Nay, friar, I am a kind of burr, I shall stick' (IV.3.177).

Mariana

'What a merit were it in death to take this poor maid from the world!' (III.1.231–2) Isabella exclaims when she hears of the fate of the deserted Mariana. But Shakespeare and the Duke require her for their plot. Clearly we are not to accuse her of unchastity in agreeing with the proposal; the pre-contract of marriage rules this out, as the Duke explains, and the heroine of Shakespeare's *All's Well that Ends Well* takes the same action to secure her husband. Yet her ready compliance, her willingness to put on the 'destin'd livery' of frail womanhood, show that she is not cut out to play the heroine. Partly this is because Shakespeare does not want her to rival Isabella for our attention, but it is in keeping with her character, essentially passive but willing to act for the man she loves. Although lightly sketched, she has a real part to play, and in the final scene speaks with a warmth and simplicity which compare favourably with Isabella:

> They say best men are moulded out of faults,
> And, for the most, become much more the better
> For being a little bad. So may my husband. (V.1.437–9)

Pompey

In a summary of the play Pompey's part will not seem a large one, though it is longer than Claudio's, and may be dismissed as 'comic relief'. Yet the scene with Escalus and Elbow (Act II Scene 1), coming immediately before the first interview between Angelo and Isabella, is no less concerned with the human realities underlying the law's abstractions. The law defines Pompey as a criminal, but he is rather, as he says, 'a poor fellow that would live' (II.1.220). His objections to the unpracticality of the extreme measures Angelo is pursuing cannot be disputed: 'Does your worship mean to geld and splay all the youth of the city?' (II.1.227–8). His conversion to hangman ironically suggests the only kind of reform of which he is capable, and also that there is no absolute distinction between the criminal and the legal apparatus which punishes him.

Escalus

He is the Duke's loyal and trusted officer and the kind of character who in Shakespeare's plays we too can trust. He is genuinely concerned for Claudio's fate and his tolerance is contrasted with Angelo's severity, though he also recognises the need for laws and penalties:

'Mercy is not itself, that oft looks so' (II.1.280). It is a mistake to play his scene with Pompey to show him bettered by the bawd. He understands the case well enough, and matches Pompey's humour while retaining his own dignity. The criminal is given good advice and another chance, but arrested when he fails to profit by it. Escalus's handling of Elbow shows a similar sympathetic common sense.

Elbow

Shakespeare's attempt to repeat the success he had had with another simple constable, Dogberry in *Much Ado About Nothing*. Elbow has a similar difficulty with words and shows the same well-meaning incompetence, though like Dogberry he is finally allowed to succeed: he manages to arrest Pompey at the second attempt.

Mistress Overdone

Her concern for Claudio and kindness to Kate Keepdown and her child remind us that the lower orders have human virtues as well as vices, but we are not allowed to invest enough interest in her to be troubled by her fate.

The Provost

The officer in charge of the prison, he is memorable for his concern for Claudio and his kindness to the pregnant Juliet, though he remains a loyal servant and is only persuaded to disobey the orders for the execution when shown the Duke's authority. He is remembered in the final speech, where his 'care and secrecy' win for him the promise of a 'worthier place' (V.1.527-8).

Barnardine

When rereading the play we may be surprised by how small a part Barnardine has. Since Ragozine, the dead pirate, eventually provides the head which is sent to Angelo in place of Claudio's, he is not strictly necessary at all. Yet his approach to death, given us in the Provost's words, is related to the two great speeches on death in Act III Scene 1:

> A man that apprehends death no more dreadfully but as a drunken sleep; careless, reckless, and fearless of what's past, present, or to come: insensible of mortality, and desperately mortal. (IV.2.140-3)

This sub-human indifference is quite unlike a mature resignation advocated by the Duke, while his unwillingness to die when it comes to the point is a kind of comic coda to Claudio's reluctance. He is indeed 'unfit to live or die!' (IV.3.63), but not beyond the Duke's mercy.

Plot and structure

Characters in comedies rarely have the determining force of characters in tragedies. By Act III Scene 1 we have seen nothing in the nature of the characters to prevent the play ending as a tragedy. They are rescued by the plot, by the Duke's plot, in the first instance, itself a part of Shakespeare's larger plot. To object to this is to quarrel with comedy itself, or at least with the romantic comedy which is Shakespeare's preferred form even in a play like this which shares some features with Jonson's satirical comedy. In the privileged world of comedy characters are protected from the consequences of weaknesses which in a tragedy would destroy them. Since in the real world there is no such protection, comedy is perhaps the more artificial form, and the artificiality is part of our enjoyment. The plot must work smoothly, but if it were completely invisible, part of our pleasure would be lost. Our sympathy for individual characters is balanced against our recognition of the pattern in which they are involved.

For his play Shakespeare ingeniously combines three separate plots:

the sister's dilemma in the face of the corrupt judge who has power over her brother's life (the story he found in Whetstone); the disguised ruler who goes among his people to know them better; and the 'bed-trick', where one woman takes the place of another in the man's bed. None of them is necessarily related to the others; in *The Changeling* (acted 1624; published 1653) by Thomas Middleton (*c*.1570–1627), for example, the bed-trick is used so that the wife can avoid her husband's bed and so conceal her lost virginity. Yet Shakespeare makes a true marriage of these disparate elements, so that the concern with justice and mercy underlying the ruler's disguise is tested in the relationship between the sister and the corrupt judge, and the difference between the judge's principles and practice is illustrated through his involvement in the bed-trick.

Not only does Shakespeare skilfully dovetail these elements, he compresses the whole action into a few days. He is never particularly concerned with the classical unities derived from the Greek philosopher Aristotle (*c*.384–322BC), who thought that the actions of a play should have no digressions, that it should take place in one setting, and that its actions should not cover a period longer than twenty-four hours. But *Measure for Measure* comes closer to observing these three unities of action, place and time than do many of the plays. As usual with Shakespeare, indications of time within the play if taken literally produce inconsistencies. When tension and urgency are required the action is hurried on, while it is still assumed that enough time has elapsed for necessary developments in the plot, like the Duke's supposed journey abroad and letters home.

The plot generates meaning through a series of parallels which the audience compares and contrasts. Angelo condemns Claudio for sleeping with Juliet, then attempts to do the same thing himself with Isabella. Isabella begs mercy for Claudio from Angelo, yet denies her brother a hearing. Later still she begs mercy for Angelo from the Duke. Angelo is guilty of the same relationship with Mariana (cohabitation on a pre-contract of marriage, but without the formal ceremony) for which he has condemned Claudio. Isabella refuses to surrender her virginity to Angelo, yet persuades Mariana to surrender hers. The Duke's impressive speech on death is immediately followed by Claudio's still more impressive plea for life. Angelo's trial of Claudio is followed by Escalus's hearing of Froth and Pompey. Angelo deserts Mariana, and Lucio abandons Kate Keepdown; both are obliged to keep their promises of marriage. These patterns we can see in abstract terms as the elaboration of the themes of the play. Isabella's commitment to mercy is revealed as no less easily shaken than Angelo's commitment to justice.

In order to appreciate these parallels we must have a more comprehensive view of the action than any of the characters except the

50 · Commentary

Duke, whose attitude, F. R. Leavis has argued, '*is* meant to be ours'.*
When the Duke is deceived, in believing that Angelo would pardon
Claudio as he had promised, we are deceived too. We may feel that
Shakespeare expects us to have some criticisms of the Duke, but it
remains true that his presence helps us to take a relatively detached view,
since we can count on him to see that no real harm is done. In case we
should miss the parallels, Shakespeare constantly draws attention to
them in the dialogue. Escalus asks Angelo:

> Whether you had not sometime in your life
> Err'd in this point, which now you censure him? (II.1.14–5)

Angelo answers:

> When I that censure him do so offend,
> Let mine own judgement pattern out my death. (II.1.29–30)

Isabella urges Angelo:

> Go to your bosom,
> Knock there, and ask your heart what it doth know
> That's like my brother's fault. (II.2.137–9)

Soon after, Angelo recognises his guilty desires:

> And in my heart the strong and swelling evil
> Of my conception. (II.4.6–7)

The Duke appears to reject Isabella's charges against Angelo in the final
scene, but in words that bring them home to the audience and to Angelo
himself:

> If he had so offended,
> He would have weigh'd thy brother by himself,
> And not have cut him off. (V.1.113–15)

This constant balancing or 'measuring' is built into the texture of the
play, but also governs the main structural movement. Nigel Alexander
in his short book on the play has shown that if we look at the scenes into
which the action is naturally separated, rather than the arbitrary
divisions of the First Folio text, we find sixteen scenes in all. Eight of
these lead up to the pivotal moment when Angelo demands the
'monstrous ransom' of Isabella, and eight show us the Duke saving the
play from the threatened tragedy.† In the first half, Lucio leads Isabella
to Angelo; in the second, the Duke and Isabella lead Mariana to Angelo.

---

*F. R. Leavis, *The Common Pursuit*, Chatto, London, 1952, p. 163.
†Nigel Alexander, *Shakespeare: Measure for Measure*, Edward Arnold, London, 1975, pp. 12–13.

The first half ends with Isabella refusing to save Claudio; the second ends with her kneeling to save Angelo.

The last act is a separate unit within this larger structure, but recapitulates the movement of the whole play. It begins with the Duke in office, as we first met him in Act I, deputing power to Angelo to judge a case which he refuses to recognise as involving himself. Again the Duke adopts the disguise of friar, and again he is attacked by Lucio. Again Isabella appeals to the judge without success, and again Mariana is rejected by Angelo. Where Mariana had helped Isabella to save her brother, Isabella is now called on to help Mariana save her husband. Where Angelo had asked for love in return for her brother's life, now it is the Duke who asks; the proposal is repeated but this time in a form she can accept. Finally the Duke resumes his rightful place and the deaths which the first half of the play seemed to threaten give way to marriages.

Language

John Dryden (1631-1700) described *Measure for Measure* as 'meanly written', and it is true that it is not a play to which we should turn first to illustrate the beauty of Shakespeare's poetry. Yet it is one of the mature plays with only the great tragedies and late romances to follow. Claudio's speech in Act III Scene 1 where the reality of death forces from him a language full of physical density reminds us of *Hamlet* but points forward to *Macbeth*. The imagined future is created in very solid terms. Even the 'viewless winds' (line 123) are transformed to 'imprison' the 'delighted spirit' (line 120). The grave offers no rest, but only 'cold obstruction' (line 118). In contrast, the Duke's speech earlier in the same scene dissolves the actuality in shifting negatives and abstractions:

> Thou hast nor youth, nor age,
> But as it were an after-dinner's sleep
> Dreaming on both; (lines 32-4)

The body, which for Claudio is instinct with 'sensible warm motion' (line 119), becomes merely 'many a thousand grains/That issue out of dust' (lines 20-1), a view which requires the detachment of the philosopher or the older man. Claudio cannot see his body as a 'habitation' (line 10); it is inseparable from his sense of his own identity.

Angelo's language at the outset is rational and logical, metaphors occurring only as deliberately chosen examples to enforce a generalisation:

> The jewel that we find, we stoop and take't,
> Because we see it; but what we do not see,
> We tread upon, and never think of it. (II.1.24-6)

Once blood gets the better of reason, abstract language gives way to richly metaphorical expression. It is not the 'idea' of Isabella which replaces his 'idea' of upright Christian lawfulness:

> Heaven in my mouth,
> As if I did but only chew his name,
> And in my heart the strong and swelling evil
> Of my conception. (II.4.4–7)

Isabella's natural expression is heavily rhetorical; as Claudio realises 'she hath prosperous art/When she will play with reason and discourse' (I.2.174–5). Her well-balanced phrases when she presents her case to Angelo remind us of another would-be lawyer, Portia in Shakespeare's *The Merchant of Venice*:

> Not the king's crown, nor the deputed sword,
> The marshal's truncheon, nor the judge's robe,
> Become them with one half so good a grace
> As mercy does. (II.2.60–3)

Indignation increases her eloquence but turns it strident and hysterical, no longer to make nice distinctions but to denounce others:

> Die, perish! Might but my bending down
> Reprieve thee from thy fate, it should proceed.
> I'll pray a thousand prayers for thy death;
> No word to save thee. (III.1.143–6)

All the examples considered so far might come under the heading of psychological realism, but Shakespeare uses language for other purposes. Sometimes he separates a passage from the more or less realistic context in which it appears by means of rhyme or a different metrical form. The audience is thus invited to generalise their experience of the play, and for a moment at least to consider the themes rather than the characters who are serving to illustrate them. The obvious example is the Duke's speech at the end of Act III Scene 2:

> He who the sword of heaven will bear
> Should be as holy as severe: (lines 254–5)

We are not to imagine the Duke musing to himself here in any realistic fashion, but as speaking directly to the audience, reminding them of the significance of what they are seeing:

> So disguise shall by th'disguised
> Pay with falsehood false exacting,
> And perform an old contracting. (lines 273–5)

The characters' language will also vary according to the circumstances.

The public speeches of Isabella and Mariana in the final act are more formal than their conversation in private.

Prose

In Shakespeare's plays characters from the lower classes of society usually speak prose, and this is the case with *Measure for Measure*. Lucio, as the friend both of the noble Claudio and the bawd Pompey, speaks verse and prose. But there are no fixed rules, and the upper-class characters speak prose too, especially in the second half of the play. In fact the increased use of prose after the middle of Act III Scene 1 is sometimes connected with a general falling-off in quality. The prosaic working-out of the plot, critics have argued, takes over from genuine inspiration. The editors of the New Cambridge edition of *Measure for Measure* suggest that the play was extensively revised, possibly by some other author who turned Shakespeare's verse into prose. This is what they have to say of the scene between Lucio and the two gentlemen (Act I Scene 2):

> Sheer mud, dreary, dead. Let the reader consider these 57 lines of prose in isolation, and ask himself if Shakespeare could have written them, at any period of his career.*

Yet there is plenty of good prose in the play, especially from Lucio, and if the play was revised, there is nothing which on internal evidence alone, the only kind we have, could not have been written by Shakespeare.

Imagery

The use of recurrent imagery to convey the themes of the play, which we find later in *Macbeth* and *King Lear,* is much less apparent in *Measure for Measure*. The corrupt nature of the city is suggested in the association of sex with disease in the conversation of Lucio and the two gentlemen, and of sex with sin in the soliloquies of Angelo, but it is not maintained throughout the play. Shakespeare in his desire to show that sexuality can have positive associations, those of fertility and plenty, gives Lucio lines in his encounter with Isabella which are scarcely in character (I.4.40–4). 'Blood' in the sense of natural emotion and sexual passion is repeatedly connected with Angelo: he 'scarce confesses/That his blood flows' (I.3.51–2); he is 'a man whose blood/Is very snow-broth' (I.4.57–8); 'the resolute acting of your blood' (II.1.12); 'Blood, thou art blood' (II.4.15) and so on. In *The Structure of Complex Words,* William Empson traces

---

*William Shakespeare, *Measure for Measure*, Ed. A. Quiller-Couch and J. Dover Wilson, Cambridge University Press, Cambridge, 1922, p. 107.

the progress of the word 'sense' through the play, seeing *Measure for Measure* as amongst other things 'a sort of examination of the word as a whole, of all that it covers in the cases where it can be used rightly' (p.270). As we should expect, the words 'justice','mercy', 'grace', 'authority', 'liberty', and 'restraint' are recurrent, and critics have noticed the connection between Isabella's angry taunt to Claudio, 'Mercy to thee would prove itself a bawd' (III.1.149), and the equivocal nature of her own action in eventually saving her brother by bringing Mariana to Angelo's bed.

The play

Having examined some of the elements that make up the whole we can ask what kind of play *Measure for Measure* is. A tragi-comedy, possibly; we know that there was a fashion for this genre around the turn of the century, though it is sometimes claimed that for the playwrights of the time tragi-comedy would have some connection with a pastoral setting, or a darker tone and more surprising reversals than we find in *Measure for Measure*. Yet it does meet many of the requirements set out in John Fletcher's definition of the form. Fletcher (1579–1625) was to become the principal writer for the King's Men after Shakespeare's retirement:

> A tragi-comedy is not so called in respect of mirth and killing, but in respect it wants deaths, which is enough to make it no tragedy, yet brings some near it, which is enough to make it no comedy, which must be a representation of familiar people, with such kind of trouble as no life be questioned ...

('Epistle to the Reader', *The Faithful Shepherdess,* 1610)

Though the Duke's presence reassures us, the play does involve a number of surprises and reversals: Angelo's fall, Isabella's harshness, her plea for his life 'against all sense' as the Duke puts it (V.1.431). *Measure for Measure* has often been found too dark for a comedy, and such a view lies behind the modern classification of 'problem play', first suggested by F. S. Boas*. For some the problem was Shakespeare's own, his difficulty in dramatising conflicts and disturbances which he could not resolve in his private life. We hear this argument less often nowadays; although Angelo and Isabella may have problems in coming to terms with their own sexuality, Shakespeare's handling of the characters seems clear and consistent, with no sign of distortion as a result of some neurosis of his own.

The other meaning of problem play, a play in which characters are faced with moral choices which bring home to the audience the problematic nature of such decisions, is more generally accepted as true

*F. S. Boas, *Shakespeare and his Predecessors*, John Murray, London, 1896.

of *Measure for Measure*. Even so, it is sometimes objected that this is to take the play too seriously. Such is the view taken by Josephine Waters Bennett in her book *Measure for Measure as Royal Entertainment*,* where she argues that we should enjoy the dilemmas of the characters without imagining that they could really happen. It is useful to be reminded that the play is entertainment and not moral instruction, but although Elizabethan law did not execute fornicators, audiences then and now would be uncomfortably aware that laws have condemned men for scarcely better reasons. We do not find it difficult to believe that in the Vienna of the play such a law could exist, and the comedy partly depends on the grim incongruousness of the punishment Angelo proposes. As Lucio protests, 'Why, what a ruthless thing is this in him, for the rebellion of a codpiece to take away the life of a man!' (III.2.110–12). Such a law may have no exact counterpart in our lives, but in the scene between Claudio and Isabella in Act III it gives rise to a display of emotions that we recognise as painfully real. Our confidence in the Duke's overall control keeps our own emotions in check, and yet we are still disturbed because the characters do not behave in a conventional way, either the brother bravely laying down his life for his sister's honour, or the heroine nobly sacrificing her chastity to let him live (the case in Whetstone's play).

The Duke makes no judgement on the exchange he has overheard. He commends Isabella for her honesty, in rather formal terms: 'the hand that hath made you fair hath made you good' (III.1.179–80). He then gets on with the practical solution to their difficulties. Although the ideal pattern of behaviour can be stated in general terms, as in his speech at the end of Act III Scene 2, he and Shakespeare are rather unwilling to pronounce on the less than ideal behaviour of ordinary people. This, after all, is the moral of the whole play, if we must reduce it to a sentence: Judge not, that ye be not judged.

Interpretations of the play as a morality, or a religious allegory, risk making this reduction, illuminating though they often are. It could even be argued that for a play where the heroine is a nun, and the central character a moral reformer who spends most of his time disguised as a friar, the atmosphere is surprisingly secular. Mariana's name may refer to Mary the virgin and Anna the immaculate mother, but it is her 'violent and unruly' (III.1.243) love for Angelo which helps to resolve the plot. The play has been seen as according to virginity an almost mystical value, but Mariana's role is more than a dramatic convenience. Her secular love, which has withstood Angelo's unkindness, proves more useful than Isabella's chastity, heroically though that has been asserted.

---

*Josephine Waters Bennett, *Measure for Measure as Royal Entertainment*, Columbia University Press, New York, 1966.

The play is certainly a comedy, but not one that promotes a detached superiority in the audience. The ending belongs to the realm of comic convention, and satisfies expectations we have had from the beginning, yet it has a muted quality when compared with the endings of some of the earlier festive comedies. This is partly because some of the leading characters, especially Angelo and Isabella, have very little to say, and partly because the pattern of marriages, when we examine it, is quite unusual. Claudio and Juliet raise no problems, but Angelo and Mariana give pause for thought, and the Duke and Isabella have given no hint of any possible romantic attachment. Isabella does not give the Duke an answer, and in a production at Stratford-upon-Avon in the 1960s he turned away a disappointed man, to bear the cares of office alone. Since Shakespeare would have been involved in producing the play in 1604, the apparently open ending must have been resolved in one way or the other, and the force of the convention whereby the Duke and Isabella marry would be almost impossible to resist; perhaps for this reason he had no need to spell it out. The way it is handled means that we recognise the rightness of the match without having to pretend an enthusiasm which nothing we have seen of the characters could justify.

Lucio views the prospect of marriage as 'whipping and hanging' (V.1.521). Indeed his punishment, enforced marriage to a known prostitute, has often been seen as disproportionate to his crime, and as casting an ironic light over marriage as an institution, or at least as a comic convention. Yet at the end of *As You Like It*, as Jacques tells us, the marriage of Touchstone and Audrey seems destined to wrangling. Shakespeare has no wish to spoil the wedding celebrations, his marriages simply illustrate the 'real state of sublunary nature'. In his plays comedy is not opposed to reality but is reality itself under one of its aspects.

Part 4

Hints for study

Approaching the play

We should remember that in the text of a play we have something less than the whole experience. One critic described the climax of a famous production in 1951 as follows:

> Mariana has passionately implored Isabella to kneel to the Duke for Angelo's pardon; the Duke has warned her that to do so would be 'against all sense' – 'He dies for Claudio.' The pause that followed must have been among the longest in theatre history. Then hesitantly, still silent, Isabella moved across the stage and knelt before the Duke. Her words came quiet and level, and as their full import of mercy reached Angelo, a sob broke from him. It was perfectly calculated and perfectly timed; and the whole perilous manoeuvre had been triumphantly brought off. (Richard David, '*Measure for Measure* on the Modern Stage'*)

Neither Isabella's long silence nor Angelo's sob are in the text as we read it, but they make the moment on stage.

We need to recognise that the play is a very specialised mixture of convention and realism, so that we must constantly adjust our expectations. If we are to enjoy the game we need to learn the rules as we go along. So, for example, we might reasonably be troubled by the 'bed-trick' because it casts doubt on Isabella's moral scruples, but it would be unreasonable to object that even in the dark Angelo must have been able to tell the difference between Isabella and Mariana. This, like the Duke's disguise, we accept with what Coleridge called 'that willing suspension of disbelief for the moment, which constitutes poetic faith'. In fact the process is not difficult, since Shakespeare expertly directs our attention to what should concern us, and away from what we need not question.

So at the outset, the Duke's pretended departure is necessary to get the play started and is recognisable as the kind of thing dukes do in fairy stories more often than in real life, yet Shakespeare does not seem to want us to accept it unquestioningly. The Duke in his conversation with Friar Thomas offers two explanations, the need to reform the laws and

**Shakespeare Survey*, IV, 1951, p. 137.

the desire to test Angelo, and we go on into the play wondering which matters more, and what is the connection between them. Our curiosity about both Angelo and the Duke is provoked by Shakespeare's handling of the incident.

Having read the play once for the story, we read it again with an eye to the themes which interested the dramatist. Since Shakespeare's audience had no opportunity to read over the play, he gives us clear signposts to the direction he is taking. Act I Scene 3 ends with the Duke's words 'Hence we shall see/If power change purpose, what our seemers be'. So we are on the look-out for discrepancies between appearance and reality in Angelo's behaviour, and since the lines are immediately followed by Isabella's first entry and her desire for 'a more strict restraint' (I.4.4) we may extend the same attention to her.

Often these directions to the audience come at the end of a scene, when some pause in the action gives us time to note them, or are made memorable by rhyme or a compressed, epigrammatic form. Angelo's first meeting with Isabella ends with the lines 'Ever till now/When men were fond, I smil'd and wonder'd how' (II.2.186–7). Isabella's dilemma is expressed in an easily remembered couplet:

Then, Isabel live chaste, and brother, die:
More than our brother is our chastity. (II.4.183–4)

As the play proceeds we come to recognise the meaning of the title, and so we are ready when it is finally quoted by the Duke in the last act, again in a rhyming couplet.

Since we have the opportunity to read the play several times, we shall probably find more and more details beginning to cluster around the main themes. The opening of Act I Scene 2 at first may seem casual comedy. Lucio and the two gentlemen joke about the pirate who keeps the Ten Commandments, except for the commandment not to steal, and the soldier who is reluctant to pray for peace. Yet in drawing attention to the difficulties and inconsistencies involved in a strict obedience to the letter of the moral law, they touch on a subject which is central to the play.

Repeated readings will also help us to notice certain key terms, such as mercy, justice, grace and blood, which recur in different contexts. We shall discover that some scenes are crucial and shall want to read them with special care, scenes like Isabella's interviews with Angelo, and then with Claudio, or her final request that the Duke pardon his sinful deputy.

Selecting quotations

Most works of literature when reduced to generalised summary seem commonplace and empty. Their power lies in their particular words, and we need to remember this when discussing them, so that we can keep as close to the text as possible while attaining the detachment necessary for criticism. Quotation is useful here, and our notes on the play should include lines and passages which encapsulate the action around them. A convenient way of arranging these is in relation to the characters. Although our impression of the characters is based on their behaviour, the compression needed for drama means that we are often given direct information about them by other characters, or in the form of soliloquies. Characters in soliloquies always tell the truth about themselves, but some comments on their fellows are more reliable than others. We should believe Escalus rather than Lucio, although Lucio's phrase about 'the old fantastical Duke of dark corners' (IV.3.156) adds to the air of mystery that surrounds the Duke.

Other quotations are worth noting not for their connection with particular characters, but to underline themes and issues which we need to consider. An example might be Lucio's 'Why, what a ruthless thing is this in him, for the rebellion of a codpiece to take away the life of a man!' (III.2.110–12). We accept Lucio's view of the unreasonable severity of the law, while hesitating to see sexual promptings and their potentially destructive effect as no more than 'the rebellion of a codpiece'. We can contrast it with other comments on the same theme, like Claudio's regret that too much liberty has cost him his freedom, or with Angelo's identification of the sexual impulse with sin:

> Most dangerous
> Is that temptation that doth goad us on
> To sin in loving virtue. (II.2.181–3)

Elsewhere Lucio himself suggests that the temptation is not simply 'rebellion', but obedience to another more natural law, which has its own validity and power:

> as blossoming time
> That from the seedness the bare fallow brings
> To teeming foison, even so her plenteous womb
> Expresseth his full tilth and husbandry. (I.4.41–4)

Our final view will depend on balancing these contrasting attitudes, rather than dismissing any of them out of hand.

Topics for study

The moral or meaning of the play

What does the title mean? What kind of justice does the play appear to advocate? What is its relationship with mercy? Is it about government? Or self-government? What does the play have to say on the subject of sex? Or on death? Are our feelings of justice 'grossly wounded' by Angelo's pardon? Does the play argue for chastity or for charity? Do the ends justify the means? Can the Duke legitimately use 'falsehood' against Angelo's 'false exacting' (III.2.274)? Can Isabella legitimately ask Mariana to take her place in Angelo's bed?

The kind of play

Is it a tragedy 'tortured' into a comedy? In what sense can it be considered a problem play? Is it an uneasy mixture of realism and folklore? Is it simply entertainment or a probing inquiry into moral questions? Is it a tragi-comedy? Or a religious allegory? Or a morality? Or a satire? Clearly this area overlaps with the previous one, and with the one that follows.

Plot and structure

Does the play break in two after Act III Scene 1? How does the ending relate to what has gone before? How does the second half mirror or parallel the first? Is the 'bed-trick' merely a dramatic device to rescue the heroine while evading her moral dilemma? How do the comic and serious parts of the play relate to each other? Does the substitution of the heads of Barnardine and Ragozine for Claudio's have any justification other than expediency? How does Shakespeare maintain tension in the play while assuring us of a probable happy outcome? How far are the marriages in the last act merely the conventional happy ending? What is the function of disguise in the play?

The characters

The Duke: what kind of interest should we take in him? Is he the conventional embodiment of Providence, or a realistic figure whose use of power is open to question?
Angelo: is he the villain of the piece, a conscious hypocrite, or a man with weaknesses we can share and excuse? Is he a puritan or a neurotic?
Isabella: is she a repressed prude, or, as John Ruskin (1819–1900) argued, a 'perfect woman', strong in 'virtuous truth and adamantine purity'? Or is she something in between?

Minor characters could also be studied, and we might consider Shakespeare's view of Claudio's weakness, or the contribution to the development and meaning of the play of Lucio, Pompey, or Mariana.

The language

In one sense the whole play is language, but we might be asked to consider the use of imagery to illustrate particular themes, like passion and restraint, appearance and reality, or liberty and law. References to disease could be seen as expressions of moral disorder, or the speech of the low-life characters could be contrasted with the idealism of Isabella, Angelo and Claudio. *Measure for Measure* seems less amenable to this approach than much of Shakespeare, and Derek Traversi has written of the 'restrained tonelessness of so much of this play.'*

We need not know the answer to all these questions, nor is it clear that the play provides any cut-and-dried solution to many of them, but we should be familiar with the relevant arguments. Part 3 of these notes has touched on some of them, and the works of criticism listed in Part 5 offer other opportunities. Secondary works should not be consulted until we are familiar with the play and have some ideas of our own. Knowledge of the sources, with the conventions of the period, and of other plays of Shakespeare (particularly *All's Well that Ends Well*), may be helpful, but *Measure for Measure* itself should take most of our attention.

Essay questions

(*i*) 'He begins well ... but he tails off into a stage puppet and ends a wearisome man, talking rubbish.' Discuss this view of the Duke.

(*ii*) Do you agree that in this play Shakespeare recast a stodgily moralistic story in the context of an orthodox Christian vision?

(*iii*) Isabella's marriage with the Duke has been described as a 'scandalous proceeding'. How would you defend it?

(*iv*) 'Our sympathies are repulsed and defeated in all directions.' Is this the real difficulty with the play?

(*v*) Lucio has been called 'probably the most acute intelligence in the play'. What does he contribute to our understanding of *Measure for Measure*?

(*vi*) 'A comedy wholly in an ironic mode.' Does this seem an apt description of the play?

(*vii*) Would you agree that *Measure for Measure* is concerned above all with the problem of self-knowledge?

(*viii*) 'Our feelings of justice are grossly wounded in Angelo's escape.' How would you justify his escape?

An Approach to Shakespeare, Sands & Co., London, 1938, p. 109.

(*ix*) Isabella's fall has been seen as 'deeper than Angelo's'. What do you understand by this remark?
(*x*) The final act has been called 'exquisite' and 'a dramatic failure'. How do you see it?
(*xi*) Shakespeare's use of disguise has been described as 'the most interesting single feature of *Measure for Measure*'. What kind of interest do you find in this aspect of the play?
(*xii*) How is the style appropriate to a play concerned less with action than with ideas?

Writing an essay

Elaborate introductions should be avoided, and examiners are annoyed when candidates ignore the question and simply write down whatever they can remember about the play. In the first of the sample essays below, the wording of the question is referred to at various points to guide the direction of the argument. The question is quite straightforward, requiring an account of the possible conceptions of the Duke's role and an explanation of his deficiencies as a result of discrepancies among them. Or it is possible to defend the coherence and success of the character when properly understood, and so disagree with the question, as in the following essay:

'He begins well... but he tails off into a stage puppet and ends a wearisome man, talking rubbish.' Discuss this view of the Duke.

Our understanding of *Measure for Measure* depends on our view of the Duke. If we see him as a cynical manipulator of other people's feelings, it becomes a satirical commentary on the nature of authority. If we see him as laying aside his power to atone for the sins of his people, as Christ came to Earth to redeem us, the play becomes a religious allegory. If he is a frankly theatrical contrivance, the play becomes an exercise in the conventions of the day. Whatever kind of justice we see in the play, it is of the Duke's devising.

The question allows that he 'begins well', but if we have difficulties with the Duke, they are there from the outset. We may accept his decision to step down as necessary to start the play, or as the action of the wise ruler of folklore. But then how seriously are we to take his concern to reform the city? Is it simply an excuse for testing Angelo? If not, then his behaviour at the end of the play may seem inconsistent.

Certainly many supposed inconsistencies in the Duke's behaviour can be explained. If it is argued that his knowledge of Angelo's desertion of Mariana makes it odd that the Duke should trust him with the deputyship, one bad action does not necessarily prove unfitness for office. If the Duke's approval of the bed-trick conflicts with his judgement of the offence of Claudio and Juliet, we could say that the Duke knows nothing of the 'true contract' in their case. If it is objected that he causes unnecessary suffering to Juliet, Isabella and Claudio, the answer must be that the educative process which they (and we the audience) undergo would be undermined by too early a revelation. This reminds us that the characters' actions are ultimately determined by their part in the drama.

The question suggests that in the later part of the play the Duke is merely part of the mechanism necessary to bring about the happy ending. Certain features of the presentation of the character make this interpretation possible, notably his self-effacing, rather detached view of the action. This detachment is partly a kind of realism (Bacon in his essay 'Of Great Place' describes virtue in authority as 'settled and calm'), but mainly the result of Shakespeare's primary interest in Angelo and Isabella. The Duke's role is governed by dramatic considerations, though it seems unnecessarily hard to call him a 'stage puppet'. In any case the Duke himself does develop. His boast of his immunity to the 'dribbling dart of love' proves to be mistaken.

The last act, far from revealing him as a 'wearisome man', shows him setting all to rights with great virtuosity. His final judgement involves no inconsistency with his attitude at the beginning of the play. He has never shared Angelo's harsh view of the law, and there is no evidence that he intended to revive the statute which imprisons Claudio. Angelo is specifically instructed 'to enforce or qualify the laws'. Lucio and the professional exponents of vice are punished with the Duke's approval. His final speech hardly shows him 'talking rubbish', though it does include the kind of marriages and pardons that we recognise and enjoy as part of the comedy, rather than the world outside the theatre.

Answers of the 'character study' variety, like the one above, are among the easiest, but more theoretical essays need more planning, though time must not be wasted on too much detail at this stage. For an answer like the one below we might make a list of the main points to be mentioned: (*a*) role-playing as a view of human behaviour. (*b*) 'seeming' as a theme of the play. (*c*) appearance and reality: Pompey and Mistress Overdone. (*d*) disguise as self-deception: Angelo and Isabella. (*e*) disguise as a source of irony. (*f*) disguise as a means of discovery: the Duke. (*g*) concealment leading to revelation.

Shakespeare's use of disguise has been described as 'the most interesting single feature of *Measure for Measure*'. What kind of interest do you find in this aspect of the play?

Shakespeare's plays are full of images of the stage as a reflection of the world, and of the world as a stage where 'one man in his time plays many parts'. In *Measure for Measure* this pattern governs the plot itself, and in the first act we are told that we shall see 'what our seemers be'. The city of Vienna is smothered in vice which is to be purged away so that the sickness can be identified and cured. Pompey disguises his true occupation of bawd with his job as a tapster, and Mistress Overdone's bath-house is a front for a brothel.

More subtle are the forms of disguise which prevent a person understanding his or her true nature. Angelo's reputation for virtue conceals his unkindness to Mariana and protects him in his attempt to seduce Isabella, but it also cuts him off from love and happiness and makes his life an empty show. Isabella's concern for her chastity threatens to destroy her charity, and to lead to her brother's death. Both Angelo and Isabella take refuge in special clothing, she in the nun's habit which marks her off from the world, and he in the judge's robes which 'wrench awe from fools' but hide the sinner beneath.

The characters deceive themselves and each other, but the audience sees all and is able to appreciate the irony of the situations that arise when Angelo and Isabella are at cross-purposes, or when Lucio unknowingly slanders the Duke to his face.

The Duke is, of course, the prime disguiser in the play, adopting the friar's gown to move freely through the action and into the confidence of his subjects, just as we the audience can. He is able to discover Juliet's love and penitence, Mariana's fidelity, Angelo's hypocrisy, and Isabella's integrity. Incidentally, in his encounter with Lucio, he learns that the position of ruler is not proof against false report.

The 'bed-trick' turns disguise against disguise and enables him to rescue the play from tragedy as Mariana takes Isabella's place:

So disguise shall by th'disguised
Pay with falsehood false exacting,
And perform an old contracting. (III.2.273–5)

In the last act Isabella asks the Duke 'to make the truth appear where it seems hid,/And hide the false seems true'. (V.1.69–70). But he conceals his knowledge of Claudio's survival until Angelo is brought to acknowledge true justice, and Isabella to plead for the mercy she had earlier denied. After the Duke has been unmasked by Lucio, the truth is finally revealed, the characters have to acknowledge their own natures and responsibilities, and the play ends with a promise that all mysteries will be resolved:

So bring us to our palace, where we'll show
What's yet behind that's meet you all should know. (V.1.535–6)

Part 5
Suggestions for further reading

The text

The text used in these Notes is:
LEVER, J. W. (ED.): *Measure for Measure*, (The Arden Shakespeare) Methuen, London, 1965. It includes appendices on the sources of the play.
Other editions include:
BAWCUTT, N. W. (ED.): *Measure for Measure*, (The Oxford Shakespeare) Clarendon Press, Oxford, 1991.
GIBBONS, B. (ED.): *Measure for Measure*, (The New Cambridge Shakespeare) Cambridge University Press, Cambridge, 1991.
NOSWORTHY, J. M. (ED.): *Measure for Measure*, (The New Penguin Shakespeare) Penguin Books, Harmondsworth, 1969.

Other works by Shakespeare

A reliable and widely used text in one volume is:
ALEXANDER, PETER (ED.): *The Complete Works*, Collins, London and Glasgow, 1951; paperback edition, HarperCollins, Glasgow, 1994.

General works on Shakespeare

BAYLEY, PETER: *An A·B·C of Shakespeare* (Longman York Handbooks) Longman, Harlow, 1985. New edition, 1993.
BENTLEY, G. E.: *Shakespeare: A Biographical Handbook*, Yale University Press, New Haven, 1961.
BRADBROOK, M. C.: *Shakespeare and Elizabethan Poetry*, Chatto and Windus, London, 1951.
BULLOUGH, GEOFFREY: *Narrative and Dramatic Sources of Shakespeare*, 8 vols, Routledge, London, 1956–75.
CRAIG, HARDIN: *The Enchanted Glass: Elizabethan Mind in Literature*, Oxford University Press, New York, 1936; reissued by Blackwell, Oxford, 1950.
GREER, G.: *Shakespeare*, (Past Masters) Oxford University Press, London, 1986. A good general introduction with a bibliography.

NAGLER, A. M.: *Shakespeare's Stage*, Yale University Press, New Haven, 1958.
ONIONS, C. T.: *A Shakespeare Glossary*, Clarendon Press, Oxford, 1911; revised by Robert D. Eagleson, Oxford, 1986.
SCHOENBAUM, S.: *Shakespeare: A Documentary Life*, Clarendon Press, Oxford, 1975.
TILLYARD, E. M. W.: *The Elizabethan World Picture*, Chatto and Windus, London, 1943; Penguin Books, Harmondsworth, 1963. Brief but readable background for the plays.
TRAVERSI, D. A.: *An Approach to Shakespeare*, second edition, Sands & Co., London, 1957.

Books on *Measure for Measure*

ALEXANDER, NIGEL: *Shakespeare: Measure for Measure*, Edward Arnold, London, 1975.
BENNETT, JOSEPHINE WATERS: *Measure for Measure as Royal Entertainment*, Columbia University Press, New York, 1966.
GLASS, D. J.: *Measure for Measure: The Law and the Convent*, Princeton University Press, Princeton, 1979.
LASCELLES, MARY: *Shakespeare's Measure for Measure*, Athlone Press, London, 1953.
MILES, ROSALIND: *The Problem of Measure for Measure*, Vision, London, 1976.
STEAD, C. K. (ED.): *Measure for Measure: A Casebook*, Macmillan, London, 1971.
STEVENSON, DAVID L.: *The Achievement of Shakespeare's Measure for Measure*, Cornell University Press, New York, 1966.

The most comprehensive book on the play is that by Rosalind Miles. David Stevenson's text is the best of the shorter works, Stevenson arguing that *Measure for Measure* is an ironic intellectual comedy. The Macmillan Casebook has a useful selection of essays, including the pieces by Wilson Knight, Empson, Leech and L. C. Knights listed below.

Critical essays on *Measure for Measure*

BATTENHOUSE, ROY W.: '*Measure for Measure* and Christian Doctrine of the Atonement', *PMLA*, 61, 1946.
COGHILL, NEVILL: 'Comic Form in *Measure for Measure*', *Shakespeare Survey*, 8, 1955.
EMPSON, WILLIAM: 'Sense in *Measure for Measure*', *The Southern Review*, 4, 1938. Reprinted in *The Structure of Complex Words*, Chatto and Windus, London, 1951.

KNIGHT, G. WILSON: *'Measure for Measure* and the Gospels', *The Wheel of Fire*, Oxford University Press, London, 1930; revised edition, 1959.

KNIGHTS, L. C.: 'The Ambiguity of *Measure for Measure*', *Scrutiny*, 10, 1942.

LEAVIS, F. R.: 'The Greatness of *Measure for Measure*', *Scrutiny*, 10, 1942. Reprinted in *The Common Pursuit*, Chatto and Windus, London, 1952.

LEECH, CLIFFORD: 'The Meaning of *Measure for Measure*', *Shakespeare Survey*, 3, 1950.

OWEN, L.: 'Mode and Character in *Measure for Measure*', *Shakespeare Quarterly*, 25, 1974, pp. 17–32.

There are several books on Shakespeare's problem plays with sections on *Measure for Measure*, including the following:

FOAKES, R. A.: *Shakespeare: The Dark Comedies to the Last Plays: From Satire to Celebration*, Routledge, London, 1971.

HUNTER, R. G.: *Shakespeare and the Comedy of Forgiveness*, Columbia University Press, New York, 1965.

LAWRENCE, W. W.: *Shakespeare's Problem Comedies*, Ungar, New York, 1931.

MUIR, K. and WELLS, S. (EDS): *Aspects of Shakespeare's Problem Plays*, Cambridge University Press, Cambridge, 1982.

SCHANZER, ERNEST: *The Problem Plays of Shakespeare*, Routledge, London, 1963.

THOMAS, V.: *The Moral Universe of Shakespeare's Problem Plays*, Croom Helm, London, 1987.

TILLYARD, E. M. W.: *Shakespeare's Problem Plays*, Chatto and Windus, London, 1950; paperback Penguin Books, Harmondsworth, 1993.

URE, PETER: *Shakespeare: The Problem Plays*, Writers and Their Work, Longman, for the British Council, London, 1961.

The author of these notes

JOHN SAUNDERS is a lecturer in English Literature at the University of Newcastle upon Tyne. He has degrees from the Universities of Oxford and Cambridge, and for a time taught in Italy. He has published reviews and translations in a number of magazines.

York Notes: list of titles

Choice of Poets
Nineteenth Century Short Stories
Poetry of the First World War
Six Women Poets

CHINUA ACHEBE
Things Fall Apart

EDWARD ALBEE
Who's Afraid of Virginia Woolf?

MAYA ANGELOU
I know Why the Caged Bird Sings

MARGARET ATWOOD
Cat's Eye
The Handmaid's Tale

JANE AUSTEN
Emma
Mansfield Park
Northanger Abbey
Persuasion
Pride and Prejudice
Sense and Sensibility

SAMUEL BECKETT
Waiting for Godot

ALAN BENNETT
Talking Heads

JOHN BETJEMAN
Selected Poems

WILLIAM BLAKE
Songs of Innocence, Songs of Experience

ROBERT BOLT
A Man For All Seasons

HAROLD BRIGHOUSE
Hobson's Choice

CHARLOTTE BRONTË
Jane Eyre

EMILY BRONTË
Wuthering Heights

ROBERT BURNS
Selected Poems

BYRON
Selected Poems

GEOFFREY CHAUCER
The Franklin's Tale
The Merchant's Tale
The Miller's Tale
The Nun's Priest's Tale
Prologue to the Canterbury Tales
The Wife of Bath's Tale

SAMUEL TAYLOR COLERIDGE
Selected Poems

JOSEPH CONRAD
Heart of Darkness

DANIEL DEFOE
Moll Flanders
Robinson Crusoe

SHELAGH DELANEY
A Taste of Honey

CHARLES DICKENS
Bleak House
David Copperfield
Great Expectations
Hard Times
Oliver Twist

EMILY DICKINSON
Selected Poems

JOHN DONNE
Selected Poems

DOUGLAS DUNN
Selected Poems

GEORGE ELIOT
Middlemarch
The Mill on the Floss
Silas Marner

T. S. ELIOT
Selected Poems
The Waste Land

HENRY FIELDING
Joseph Andrews

F. SCOTT FITZGERALD
The Great Gatsby

E. M. FORSTER
Howards End
A Passage to India

JOHN FOWLES
The French Lieutenant's Woman

BRIAN FRIEL
Translations

ELIZABETH GASKELL
North and South

WILLIAM GOLDING
Lord of the Flies

OLIVER GOLDSMITH
She Stoops to Conquer

GRAHAM GREENE
Brighton Rock

WILLIS HALL
The Long, The Short and The Tall
THOMAS HARDY
Far from the Madding Crowd
Jude the Obscure
The Mayor of Casterbridge
Selected Poems
Tess of the D'Urbervilles
L. P. HARTLEY
The Go-Between
NATHANIEL HAWTHORNE
The Scarlet Letter
SEAMUS HEANEY
Selected Poems
ERNEST HEMINGWAY
The Old Man and the Sea
SUSAN HILL
I'm the King of the Castle
BARRY HINES
A Kestrel for a Knave
HOMER
The Iliad
The Odyssey
ALDOUS HUXLEY
Brave New World
BEN JONSON
The Alchemist
Volpone
JAMES JOYCE
Dubliners
A Portrait of the Artist as a Young Man
JOHN KEATS
Selected Poems
PHILIP LARKIN
Selected Poems
D. H. LAWRENCE
The Rainbow
Sons and Lovers
Women in Love
LOUISE LAWRENCE
Children of the Dust
HARPER LEE
To Kill a Mockingbird
LAURIE LEE
Cider with Rosie
CHRISTOPHER MARLOWE
Doctor Faustus
ARTHUR MILLER
The Crucible
Death of a Salesman
A View from the Bridge

JOHN MILTON
Paradise Lost I & II
Paradise Lost IV & IX
TONI MORRISON
Beloved
SEAN O'CASEY
Juno and the Paycock
GEORGE ORWELL
Animal Farm
Nineteen Eighty-four
JOHN OSBORNE
Look Back in Anger
WILFRED OWEN
Selected Poems
HAROLD PINTER
The Caretaker
SYLVIA PLATH
Selected Works
ALEXANDER POPE
Selected Poems
J. B. PRIESTLEY
An Inspector Calls
JEAN RHYS
The Wide Sargasso Sea
WILLY RUSSELL
Educating Rita
Our Day Out
J. D. SALINGER
The Catcher in the Rye
WILLIAM SHAKESPEARE
Antony and Cleopatra
As You Like It
Coriolanus
Hamlet
Henry IV Part I
Henry V
Julius Caesar
King Lear
Macbeth
Measure for Measure
The Merchant of Venice
A Midsummer Night's Dream
Much Ado About Nothing
Othello
Richard II
Richard III
Romeo and Juliet
Sonnets
The Taming of the Shrew
The Tempest
Twelfth Night
The Winter's Tale

GEORGE BERNARD SHAW
Arms and the Man
Pygmalion
Saint Joan

MARY SHELLEY
Frankenstein

RICHARD BRINSLEY SHERIDAN
The Rivals

R. C. SHERRIFF
Journey's End

RUKSHANA SMITH
Salt on the Snow

MURIEL SPARK
The Prime of Miss Jean Brodie

JOHN STEINBECK
The Grapes of Wrath
Of Mice and Men
The Pearl

TOM STOPPARD
Rosencrantz and Guildenstern are Dead

ROBERT LOUIS STEVENSON
Dr Jekyll and Mr Hyde

JONATHAN SWIFT
Gulliver's Travels

ROBERT SWINDELLS
Daz for Zoe

JOHN MILLINGTON SYNGE
The Playboy of the Western World

MILDRED D. TAYLOR
Roll of Thunder, Hear My Cry

W. M. THACKERAY
Vanity Fair

MARK TWAIN
Huckleberry Finn

VIRGIL
The Aeneid

DEREK WALCOTT
Selected Poems

ALICE WALKER
The Color Purple

JAMES WATSON
Talking in Whispers

JOHN WEBSTER
The Duchess of Malfi

OSCAR WILDE
The Importance of Being Earnest

TENNESSEE WILLIAMS
Cat on a Hot Tin Roof
A Streetcar Named Desire

VIRGINIA WOOLF
Mrs Dalloway
To the Lighthouse

WILLIAM WORDSWORTH
Selected Poems

W. B. YEATS
Selected Poems

York Handbooks: list of titles

YORK HANDBOOKS form a companion series to York Notes and are designed to meet the wider needs of students of English and related fields. Each volume is a compact study of a given subject area, written by an authority with experience in communicating the essential ideas to students at all levels.

A DICTIONARY OF LITERARY TERMS (Second Edition)
by MARTIN GRAY
ENGLISH POETRY
by CLIVE T. PROBYN
AN INTRODUCTION TO LINGUISTICS
by LORETO TODD
STUDYING SHAKESPEARE
by MARTIN STEPHEN *and* PHILIP FRANKS